S0-APO-663

Chemical Dependency

Chemical Dependency

Look for these and other books in the Lucent Overview series:

Abortion
Acid Rain
Adoption
Advertising
AIDS
The Beginning of Writing
Bigotry
Cancer
Censorship
Cities
Civil Liberties
Cloning
Cults
Dealing with Death
Death Penalty
Democracy
Divorce
Drug Abuse
Drug Trafficking
Eating Disorders
Endangered Species
The End of Apartheid in South Africa
Environmental Groups
Espionage
Ethnic Violence
Gambling
Gangs
Gay Rights
Hazardous Waste
Health Care
Homeless Children

Homelessness
Human Rights
Illegal Immigration
The Internet
Juvenile Crime
Medical Ethics
Mental Illness
Militias
Money
Oil Spills
The Olympic Games
The Palestinian-Israeli Accord
Paranormal Phenomena
Police Brutality
Population
Poverty
Rap Music
The Rebuilding of Bosnia
Saving the American Wilderness
Schools
School Violence
Smoking
Sports in America
Suicide
The U.S. Congress
The U.S. Presidency
Violence Against Women
Women's Rights
World Hunger
Zoos

362.29
SHEEN

Chemical Dependency

by Barbara Sheen

LUCENT
BOOKS®

THOMSON
★
GALE

San Diego • Detroit • New York • San Francisco • Cleveland • New Haven, Conn. • Waterville, Maine • London • Munich

© 2003 by Lucent Books. Lucent Books is an imprint of The Gale Group, Inc.,
a division of Thomson Learning, Inc.

Lucent Books® and Thomson Learning™ are trademarks used herein under license.

For more information, contact
Lucent Books
27500 Drake Rd.
Farmington Hills, MI 48331-3535
Or you can visit our Internet site at http://www.gale.com

ALL RIGHTS RESERVED.
No part of this work covered by the copyright hereon may be reproduced or used in any form or by
any means—graphic, electronic, or mechanical, including photocopying, recording, taping, Web dis-
tribution or information storage retrieval systems—without the written permission of the publisher.

LIBRARY OF CONGRESS CATALOGING-IN-PUBLICATION DATA

Sheen, Barbara.
  Chemical dependency / Barbara Sheen.
    v. cm. — (Lucent overview series)
Includes bibliographical references and index.
Contents: What is chemical dependency? — Why do people become dependent on
chemicals? — The effects of chemical dependency — Treatment — Staying chemical
free — Prevention.
ISBN 1-56006-[...]-[...] (hc. : alk. paper)
  1. Substance abuse—Juvenile literature. [1. Substance abuse.] I. Title. II. Series.
RC564.3.S53 2004
362.29—dc21

2003003541

Printed in the United States of America

Contents

Introduction

D<small>ION WAS</small> THIRTEEN when he started experimenting with cigarettes, alcohol, and drugs. Although he believed using these chemicals was innocent fun, by the time he was sixteen he was addicted to cocaine. For the next four years, drugs were his main focus in life. "I was either getting high or trying to score," he explains. "I dropped out of school. I quit my job. I lied. I cheated. I stole. And, I disrespected myself and my family, just to get high. I kept telling my family I'd stop. No way that was going to happen; the coke was in control. My life was a nightmare of my own making. Talk about bad choices. Who would have thought this would happen to me?" [1]

Dion is one of more than 30 million Americans who compulsively abuse chemicals that impair their well-being. These chemicals include alcohol, tobacco, and legal and illegal drugs. Experts estimate that one out of every four Americans has a parent, child, sibling, or spouse who abuses harmful chemicals. Like Dion, all of these people began using chemicals voluntarily. Most had no idea how these chemicals would change their lives and the lives of those around them.

Chemical dependency affects people of all ages, forming a common bond among children, teenagers, adults, and senior citizens. It is a condition that does not discriminate. It affects people of all races and economic backgrounds. Chemical dependency is as common among the rich as it is among the poor and affects average working people as well as prominent celebrities.

People with a chemical dependence are robbed of their physical, mental, and emotional health. Their judgment is impaired. Families are often wrecked, and pain and heartache are inflicted on the people who are close to them.

Moreover, because chemical dependency is so widespread, its effects are far-reaching. According to estimates by the National Institute on Drug Abuse and the National Institute on Alcohol Abuse and Alcoholism the total economic cost of drug and alcohol abuse in the United States exceeds $245 billion a year. This includes the cost of substance abuse treatment and prevention programs; drug-related health care, including over a quarter of a million hospital emergency room visits each year due to drug overdoses; lost earnings; welfare payments to substance abusers; and crime caused by chemical dependency. Although about 50 percent of these costs are borne by the government, it is individual citizens who ultimately bear the expense through taxes.

A teenage girl at a substance abuse treatment center poses for a photo. Chemical dependency affects people of all ages, races, and backgrounds.

In addition to economic costs, experts estimate each chemically dependent person negatively impacts at least fifteen nonusers. These people include family members, friends, and coworkers, as well as innocent strangers who are frequently victims of drug- or alcohol-related accidents and crime. The daughter of a drug-related crime victim explains:

> My eighty-year-old mother was mugged by a junkie [a drug addict]. He knocked her down and grabbed her purse. The fall broke her wrist and her hip. That was three years ago. Because of her age, her bones never healed properly. She is confined to a wheelchair and will be for the rest of her life. Before the mugging she was very spry and independent. Now she's been forced to move in with my family. Although we love her, it is not easy. She can't even dress herself without help. My son had to give up his bedroom for her. Because we go to work, we have a nurse in during the day to look after her, and it's very expensive. Although we're all trying to make the best of a difficult situation, the reality is my mother's life was ruined by that junkie, and my family's life was changed forever.[2]

Because chemical dependency's impact is so far-reaching, it is important that people understand more about it. Moreover, since the initial decision to use chemicals is voluntary, by understanding chemical dependency, its causes, effects, and the problems created by it, people can make informed choices. This knowledge should help to limit the devastating impact chemical dependency has on individuals and society. Dion explains, "Let's face it, people wouldn't get high if it didn't feel good, right? The problem is the high doesn't last, but the grief you cause does. Would I do it all over again, if I could? No way. If I'd known then what I know now, I never would have used, never."[3]

1

What Is Chemical Dependency?

CHEMICAL DEPENDENCY IS a physical or psychological need for a chemical that is taken for nonmedical reasons and produces a noticeable effect on the body. The need is referred to as a "dependency" because once a person stops using the chemical, physical, emotional, or psychological withdrawal symptoms occur. There are a number of different chemicals, such as alcohol, tobacco, and drugs, that people become dependent upon, all of which may have a harmful effect on the user.

A progressive need

Chemical dependency is a progressive condition. That is, it begins slowly and grows until it dominates a person's life. As chemical dependency progresses, users have a hard time limiting their use of the chemical. They may feel that they cannot experience pleasure or relief from stress without the chemical and thus may develop a psychological or physical need for it.

This occurs because the brain reacts to pleasurable feelings, whether naturally or chemically induced, by trying to sustain them. Consequently, the brain signals the body to continue whatever action causes pleasurable feelings. This leads to psychological dependency. At the same time physical dependency develops as the brain adapts to the effects of the chemical by decreasing production of dopamine, a natural substance that produces feelings of pleasure. As dopamine levels drop, substance abusers must continuously increase their chemical intake in order to stimulate the brain to release enough dopamine to duplicate the chemical's original effect. What is more, due to the decrease of normal dopamine production, chemically dependent people often feel bad when they are not using the chemical. A formerly chemically dependent woman explains how this progression affected her:

> I started taking Valium [a tranquilizer] to help me relax. I was going through a very difficult time in my life and its calming effect was a lifesaver. At first I took a pill whenever I felt anxious. That quickly progressed to one a day. After a while, one a day wasn't enough. It didn't relax me, and I was taking three or four at a time. I couldn't stop. I needed those pills. Even the thought of not having them gave me a panic attack. Without them I was a basket case.[4]

The stages of chemical dependency

Experts classify the progression of chemical dependency into four stages: casual use, more frequent use, daily use, and addiction. The first stage, casual use, is an introductory stage characterized by curiosity and experimentation in which people use a chemical for the first time. Sometimes people do not progress beyond this stage. However, in cases that involve an extremely powerful chemical such as heroin, even casual use can put the user at risk of becoming addicted.

In the second stage the chemical is used at social gatherings, before specific events, or on the weekends. Because frequent use of any chemical can harm the body and lead to dependency, people who progress to this stage put themselves at risk.

When people reach the daily use stage, usage of the chemical has become an important part of their lives. As a result, they often ignore other aspects of their lives in order to get high. Naturally, such habitual use of any chemical takes a serious toll on a person's body.

Addiction characterizes the final stage. At this point, because users have developed a physical or psychological dependency on the chemical, they cannot stop using it even if they want to and, in order to cope with their bodies' growing tolerance to the chemical, they need increasingly larger amounts in order to feel well. Consequently, their need for

the chemical seems to control them. This negatively impacts the user physically, mentally, and emotionally and leads to a large number of problems.

A group of teenagers smokes cigarettes. Cigarettes or other gateway drugs often lead to experimentation with harder drugs.

Gateway drugs

The first stage of chemical dependency is often characterized by the casual use of tobacco, alcohol, or marijuana, which are known as gateway drugs. These chemicals are readily available and are considered less dangerous and less addictive than other drugs. However, they are not harmless. Moreover, their use often leads to experimentation with other substances. Statistics show that people who use tobacco, for example, are six times more likely to try other drugs than people who do not smoke. Similarly, studies show that people who experiment with marijuana are 79 percent more likely to become chemically dependent sometime in their lives than those who do not. A young man talks about his experience: "I started out drinking beer and smoking pot [marijuana]. Beer relaxed me, and pot made me laugh. They were totally harmless, right? Then my cousin scored some coke [cocaine]. I figured the beer and the pot hadn't hurt me, so why not try the coke? Right away, I loved it. I was flying. I felt so in charge, and so happy. The rest is history. For a while there, coke was my life."[5]

Tobacco

Of the three gateway drugs, tobacco is the most commonly used and most readily available. It contains nicotine, a powerful addictive chemical, which works by signaling the amyg-

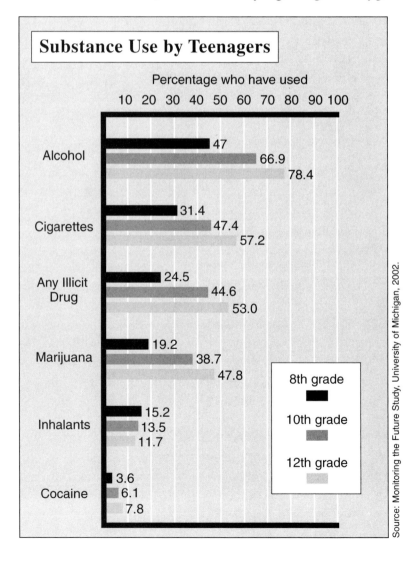

Substance Use by Teenagers

Percentage who have used

10 20 30 40 50 60 70 80 90 100

Alcohol
- 47
- 66.9
- 78.4

Cigarettes
- 31.4
- 47.4
- 57.2

Any Illicit Drug
- 24.5
- 44.6
- 53.0

Marijuana
- 19.2
- 38.7
- 47.8

Inhalants
- 15.2
- 13.5
- 11.7

Cocaine
- 3.6
- 6.1
- 7.8

8th grade
10th grade
12th grade

Source: Monitoring the Future Study, University of Michigan, 2002.

dala, or pleasure center of the brain, to secrete larger than normal amounts of dopamine. This makes users feel happy and relaxed. However, frequent use of tobacco gradually depletes the brain's normal supply of dopamine, resulting in a limited quantity of dopamine being available. Consequently, people must smoke or chew more tobacco in order for the brain to release enough dopamine for them to feel happy and relaxed. The result is addiction.

Alcohol

Like tobacco, alcohol is a legal chemical. Ingested in the form of beer, wine, or hard liquor, alcohol makes people feel relaxed and uninhibited. Alcohol affects the brain and causes addiction in the same manner as tobacco. However, because alcohol stimulates the release of even greater amounts of dopamine than tobacco does, when alcoholics are not drinking they often feel angry and irritable since their normal dopamine levels become so depleted.

Marijuana

Although the third gateway drug, marijuana, is illegal, it is considered by some people to be as socially acceptable as alcohol. In fact, experts estimate that half of the people in the United States have used it. Marijuana has not been found to be physically addictive; however, it can lead to psychological dependence because once people become accustomed to the pleasurable feelings they get from marijuana, coping with normal, less pleasurable sensations becomes increasingly difficult.

Marijuana is smoked in a pipe or cigarette and contains a chemical known as THC, which causes mood changes in the user. Depending upon the user's state of mind, it can be stimulating, relaxing, or cause hallucinations.

Other chemicals

Along with the gateway drugs, there are a number of other chemicals that people commonly become dependent upon. Like tobacco and alcohol, some are legal substances while others are illegal. These chemicals include inhalants, stimulants, depressants, hallucinogens, and anabolic steroids.

Inhalants

Inhalants are legal substances found in more than one thousand household products, including spray paint, gasoline, and model glue. When inhaled, thcsc chemicals stimulate dopamine production in the pleasure center of the brain, producing very brief feelings of euphoria. However, as in the case of alcohol and tobacco users, inhalant users must increase the frequency of their usage in order to maintain the effect. This typically results in addiction. Making matters worse, because inhalants are composed of highly toxic chemicals not designed to be absorbed into the body, other effects of inhalants include violent behavior and hallucinations.

Stimulants

Like inhalants, stimulants are powerful chemicals that, just as the name implies, stimulate users, producing feelings of strength, alertness, and exhilaration. Stimulants include caffeine and more powerful chemicals such as amphetamines, ecstasy, and cocaine. They are swallowed, inhaled, injected, and smoked. Some, such as amphetamines, are prescribed to help people lose weight or combat fatigue, but many stimulants are used illegally.

Stimulants affect the brain in a similar manner as alcohol, increasing dopamine production at first and then depleting the brain's normal supply of the substance. As a result it becomes increasingly difficult for a user to feel stimulated without the chemicals. This effect on the brain occurs very rapidly, making stimulants extremely addictive. A man who was dependent upon cocaine recalls: "It happened really fast. I was tooting up [snorting cocaine] for about two weeks. Not long enough to do any harm, or that's what I figured. But I couldn't control myself. I had to have it. I couldn't make it through a day without it. I soared on coke and felt numb without it."[6]

Depressants

Like stimulants, depressants, which include barbiturates, tranquilizers, and opiates like heroin, are prescribed legally as sleeping pills, muscle relaxants, and painkillers. Without a prescription, taking depressants is illegal. Although both stim-

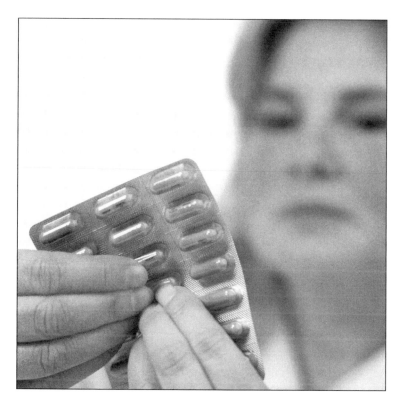

A woman opens a package of prescription pills. Patients can easily become addicted to both stimulant and depressant prescription drugs.

ulants and depressants produce intense feelings of pleasure, stimulants excite the user, whereas depressants relax the user.

Depressants affect dopamine levels in the same manner as stimulants. Similarly, because of their potency, addiction occurs rapidly. Addiction expert Elizabeth Connell Henderson explains, "When the brain is exposed to opiates, physical tolerance and dependence develop, even at very low doses. It has been shown, for example, that hospital patients who are given even small doses of opiate medication for acute pain have a mini withdrawal syndrome even after the first dose."[7]

Making matters worse, even a small overdose of depressants can lead to death. According to Henderson,

> These drugs have a low therapeutic index, meaning that the dose required for the desired effect is very close to the toxic dose. People suffering from barbiturate overdose, an extremely dangerous situation, are commonly seen in emergency rooms. Often these overdoses are accidental. The user, having developed a tolerance to the drug's sedative [relaxing] effects, would repeat the dose.[8]

Hallucinogens

Unlike the feeling of euphoria produced by stimulants and depressants, hallucinogens such as LSD and PCP cause people to experience hallucinations, or imagined experiences that seem real. Hallucinogens disrupt the action of neurotransmitters that send messages from the five senses to the brain. This causes changes in the way a person perceives the world. As a result, he or she often sees, hears, tastes, smells, or feels things that are not there. These perceptions, however, are unpredictable. If a person is feeling nervous or upset before taking a hallucinogen, he or she may experience what is known as a "bad trip," which is like a waking nightmare. In order to escape the nightmare, people often put themselves at risk. For example, people on bad trips have been known to jump from great heights or run into traffic. Furthermore, because hallucinogens are mind-altering chemicals, even when a bad trip is over, a user can experience frightening flashbacks for years to come. A former LSD user explains, "It's been more than twenty years since I dropped acid [LSD], but I still get flashbacks. I can be lying in bed, or watching TV and all of a sudden I'm tripping. If I'd known this was going to happen, I'd never have dropped acid in the first place."[9]

Although not physically addictive, because good trips can be extremely pleasurable, hallucinogens can cause psychological dependence.

Anabolic steroids

Unlike chemicals that people use in order to produce feelings of pleasure, anabolic steroids, which are synthetic copies of the hormone testosterone that the body naturally produces, are used to increase muscle strength and performance. Anabolic steroids affect the hypothalamus, the part of the brain that controls mood, appetite, and normal hormone functions. Over time, use of anabolic steroids changes the messages the hypothalamus sends to the rest of the body, and in order for users to feel strong, they must increase their steroid dosage. This can cause both physical and psychological dependence. Although steroids do make people feel physically stronger, since they affect the part of the brain that controls moods, anabolic steroid users often experience uncontrollable anger, known as "roid rage." Since steroid dependency is a serious problem, many athletic associations, including the International Olympic Committee, have banned their use and disqualify competitors who use them.

Physical effects of chemical dependency

No matter what chemical is abused, all forms of chemical dependency negatively impact the user's body. Frequent exposure to chemicals causes changes in almost every organ in a person's body and, thus, in the way the body works. For example, frequent consumption of alcohol can damage a person's liver, slow his or her heartbeat and breathing, and impair muscle coordination. Stimulants, marijuana, and hallucinogens accelerate a person's heartbeat and increase his or her blood pressure. This can lead to a heart attack or stroke.

Inhalants, too, affect heart rate. Toxic chemicals found in inhalants are not meant for human consumption and can decrease an inhalant user's heart rate to levels so low that a

Ben Johnson breaks a world record in the 1988 Olympics. After the International Olympic Committee found he used steroids, he was stripped of the record.

coma or death from cardiac arrest may occur. Experts estimate that more than one thousand deaths each year are caused by inhalant abuse and most of the victims are children. According to researcher Matthew Howard of Washington University in Saint Louis, "Surveys show that approximately one out of every five American children will experiment with inhalants before they complete eighth grade. I don't think these kids have any idea how dangerous inhaling these substances can be. Some kids don't get the message until a friend ends up dead or in the hospital." [10]

Similarly, addiction to tobacco has been linked to heart disease as well as lung diseases such as emphysema and lung cancer. In fact, according to the U.S. Center for Substance Abuse Prevention, tobacco use is responsible for more than 450,000 deaths in the United States each year. What is more, since marijuana is inhaled through the lungs, it presents similar health risks as tobacco.

Chemical dependency also weakens and damages the immune system. This makes it difficult for chemical abusers to fight off diseases. This is especially troubling since sharing drug needles and cocaine straws can expose chemically dependent people to potentially lethal viruses such as HIV and hepatitis. In fact, it is estimated that between 60 and 90 percent of all intravenous drug users are infected with hepatitis. According to infectious disease expert Dr. Mark Tyndall, "Hepatitis seems to be an occupational hazard among people who inject drugs. Amongst those who are actively using, it seems difficult to avoid hepatitis." [11] Since even a healthy immune system has trouble fighting these viruses, when they strike chemically dependent people the results are often fatal.

Emotional effects of chemical dependency

Because chemicals are powerful substances that affect the pleasure center of the brain, chemical abuse can also cause emotional problems. Using stimulants, for example, can overexcite a user and result in feelings of anxiety and nervousness. Compounding the problem, when the effects of these chemicals wear off, users go from feeling excited and happy to exhausted and irritable. In some cases, this irritabil-

Chemical dependency affects normal brain function, leading to emotional and psychological problems.

ity presents itself as aggressive and often violent behavior. A former cocaine abuser attests, "I'm not a bad guy, ask anyone. I've always been laid-back and smooth. But when I was doing coke anything could set me off, especially when I was coming down. Crashing made me mean, 'kick puppies in the shins' mean." [12]

Psychological effects of chemical dependency

The repercussions of chemical dependency on the brain do not end with emotional problems. Because chemical dependency affects the way the brain functions, mental problems such as memory loss and impaired judgment often occur. Worse yet, chemical dependency can cause brain damage. Frequent exposure to toxic chemicals in inhalants, for example, can permanently destroy brain cells and impair thinking and learning. A teacher talks about the effect of inhalants on one of her students: "He's eighteen. He started using inhalants when he was eight. At that time he was an average student of normal intelligence. Now he's classified as mentally retarded. He can no longer read or write or hold a normal conversation. Sometimes he forgets his own name. The worst part is that he did this to himself."[13]

Chemical dependency also causes psychological disorders. Large amounts of drugs change the balance of normal chemicals in the brain. Scientists theorize that this disrupts the normal working of the brain. Symptoms of mental illness, such as schizophrenia, depression, and paranoia may result. In some cases, the symptoms diminish once people stop using chemicals. However, in other cases the symptoms persist. This is particularly true in people who abuse hallucinogens, since their mind-altering effects can actually stimulate the onset of mental illnesses. A study at Mount Sinai School of Medicine in New York City investigated the long-term link between psychological disorders and chemical dependency in 736 formerly chemically dependent subjects. The study began in 1988 and concluded in 2002. Examining the results, researchers found that 8.3 percent of the subjects suffered from clinical depression, which researchers said indicated a significant link between mental illness and dependence on alcohol, marijuana, cocaine, and hallucinogens. According to researcher David W. Brook, one of the authors of the study, "The fact that we are able to predict this is new, startling, and alarming. We can take this to our patient population and we can say this usage is a predictor of future psychopathology [mental illness]."[14]

Yet despite the many problems chemicals cause, affecting the bodies, emotions, and brains of users, millions of people continue to abuse them and become chemically dependent.

2

Why Do People Become Dependent on Chemicals?

PEOPLE WHO ABUSE chemicals are influenced by both external and internal factors. The influence of a person's friends, family, or society is a common external factor that leads to chemical dependency. Coping with an emotional need or problem, on the other hand, is an internal factor that leads people to use chemicals.

Curiosity

One such internal factor is curiosity. Curiosity is often the reason that teenagers, in particular, abuse chemicals. Since the teen years are a time in which young people are trying to ascertain who they are, teenagers are apt to experiment with new things in an effort to discover more about themselves. Experimenting with chemical substances is frequently part of this process.

In most cases, when teenagers experiment with chemicals they do so under the assumption that the chemicals will have no long-term effect on them. However, studies have shown that the use of chemicals at a young age is linked to chemical dependency in the future. A 1998 study by the National Institute on Alcohol Abuse and Alcoholism found that young people who experiment with alcohol before age fifteen are four times more likely to become alcoholics by the time they are twenty-one than those who do not. Experts say that the link

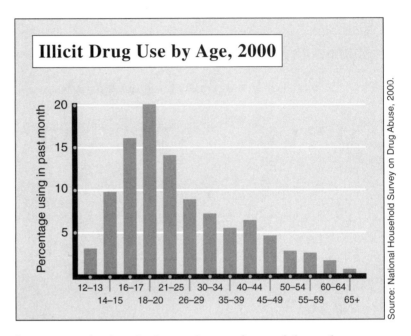

Illicit Drug Use by Age, 2000

Percentage using in past month

20
15
10
5

12–13 16–17 21–25 30–34 40–44 50–54 60–64
14–15 18–20 26–29 35–39 45–49 55–59 65+

Source: National Household Survey on Drug Abuse, 2000.

between early chemical experimentation and dependency occurs because a teenager's body is still developing and does not have the same capacity to handle the effects of chemicals as does an adult's body.

Thrill-seeking behavior

Another internal factor that influences both teenagers and adults to abuse chemicals is thrill-seeking behavior. Thrill-seeking behavior involves people abusing chemicals in an effort to make their lives more exciting. People in this group are often bored or rebellious, turning to chemicals such as amphetamines, alcohol, marijuana, cocaine, and hallucinogens in an attempt to add more excitement to their lives. These chemicals provide people with a physical rush. In addition, because these are illegal substances, by abusing them thrill-seekers gain the additional excitement of committing a crime without, they think, much chance of getting caught. However, this is not always the case. A man talks about the reasons for his thrill-seeking behavior and how it resulted in his being arrested:

> I grew up in a town you could fit in your back pocket. It was right in the middle of nowhere, surrounded by nothing. There was no

mall, no movies, no nothing. Sometimes it was like a person could just about die from the boredom, same old people, same old stories, same old, same old. Drinking helped pass the time, so did smoking a few joints. Dropping acid really took me to another place, made life a little more exciting. So did the additional rush of breaking the law. But getting busted when I was sixteen was more excitement than I bargained for.[15]

Easing emotional pain

Whereas people who are influenced by curiosity and thrill-seeking abuse chemicals in an effort to have fun, in other cases people become dependent on chemicals in order to escape from their personal problems. One typical problem is low self-esteem. People who suffer from low self-esteem feel that they do not measure up to the standards of others. This often causes them to feel insecure or shy around other people. Consequently, they frequently use chemicals such as alcohol, marijuana, and tranquilizers in an effort to lessen their anxiety and inhibitions and to help them to forget how bad they feel about themselves. According to experts at the insurance company BlueCross BlueShield of Texas, "A person with low self-esteem may feel they are not as smart, attractive, talented or popular as their peers. They may also feel pressured to achieve goals that seem unattainable. To help deal with this pressure, a person with low self-esteem may be more likely to put aside his/her good judgment and turn to drugs or alcohol to escape."[16]

Depression

Like low self-esteem, depression is another emotional problem that many people deal with by abusing chemicals. When people suffer from depression they feel sad, disinterested in daily life, anxious, and fatigued. Abusing chemicals such as cocaine, alcohol, and opiates that stimulate the pleasure center of the brain and change a person's mood help mask these symptoms. Consequently, many depressed people abuse drugs and alcohol in order to cope with their problem. According to the American Society of Addiction Medicine, depressed people are more than twice as likely to abuse chemicals than people who do not suffer from depression. However, unlike psychotherapy and prescribed medication that are designed to be long-term treatments for depression, self-medicating to deal with depression yields only short-term results. Therefore, people who abuse illegal chemicals to cope with depression must take more and more in order to get long-term relief.

Loneliness

Coping with loneliness is another emotional problem that often leads people to become dependent on chemicals. When people have no one to talk to or share their experiences with, they often turn to chemicals to ease their pain. This especially affects the elderly who may have lost a spouse or been forced to move from a beloved home, leaving old friends behind. This makes them feel socially isolated. In many inci-

Depression can cause people to abuse chemicals to elevate their moods. The resulting chemical dependency can lead to even more severe depression.

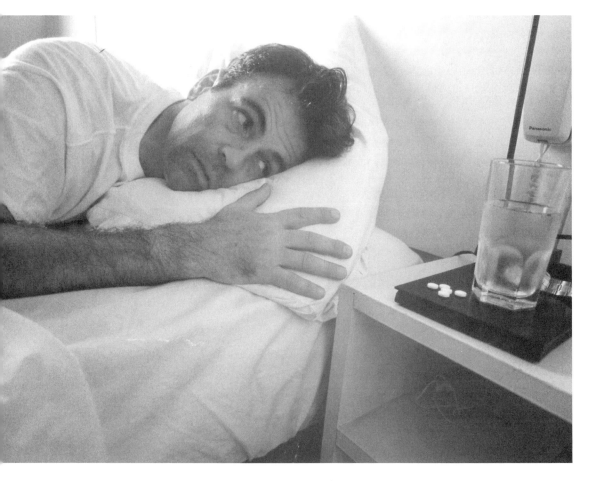

Many elderly people, like the woman pictured here, drink alcohol to cope with their loneliness. The elderly are particularly susceptible to dependence on alcohol.

dences, the impact on their emotional state is so great that it interferes with their daily life and their ability to sleep. Consequently, many elderly people turn to alcohol to cope with their loneliness. In fact, an estimated 2.5 million older Americans are alcoholics. According to experts, "Someone who has been a teetotaler [nondrinker] all his or her life may start drinking alcohol just 'to help me get some sleep.' After the death of a spouse, some people may find the need to drink alcohol to 'just get through the day.'"[17]

Abusing alcohol is not the only way this group deals with loneliness. Many elderly people mix alcohol with other chemicals such as tranquilizers. Since a large share of legal prescription medication for older people is for tranquilizers, prescribed to help alter their mood or help them sleep, the elderly have easy access to these drugs. However, many older people are not using tranquilizers as prescribed. According to a survey by the Center for Substance Abuse Treatment in California, 17 percent of Americans over sixty are addicted to tranquilizers.

Stress

Like loneliness, stress is another emotional problem that people try to solve by abusing chemicals. When people are under stress they often turn to chemicals in an effort to relax or escape.

A number of studies have found a strong connection between stress and chemical abuse. One animal study at Louisiana State University in 2001 found that stress promotes drug abuse in rats. In this study three groups of rats were

Post-traumatic stress resulting from events like those of September 11, 2001, can lead to chemical dependency.

placed in a cage in which they could press a bar to receive intravenous doses of cocaine and amphetamines. One group of rats received a mild shock to their feet that stressed them physically. The second group of rats were stressed psychologically when they witnessed this action. The third, a control group, were not stressed in any way. As the scientists expected, the more the first two groups were stressed, the more often they pressed the bar to receive the drugs, whereas the control group showed little interest in the drugs.

Another study conducted at Johns Hopkins University in Maryland in 2001 looked at the connection between high-stress jobs and chemical dependency. This study found that nurses who work in a stressful environment are one and a half times more likely to abuse cocaine and marijuana than nurses who work in a low stress environment. Researcher and drug expert Nicholas Goeders explains,

> If certain individuals are more sensitive to stress, especially if they are in an environment where they feel they have inadequate control over this stress, then these individuals may be more likely to use cocaine and other drugs of abuse. This could occur whether the person is an executive in a high-level stress position or a teenager living in a low-income, inner-city environment with no hope of ever advancing.[18]

Post-traumatic stress

In addition to the stress of everyday life, post-traumatic stress, a form of stress that develops in people after witnessing or participating in a life-threatening event, often leads to chemical dependency. Serious accidents, military combat, natural disasters, and physical or sexual assault all can cause post-traumatic stress. When people suffer from post-traumatic stress they repeatedly re-experience the original trauma and frequently turn to chemicals in order to escape.

Experts estimate that between 30 and 60 percent of all chemically dependent individuals suffer from post-traumatic stress. Because of this link, the National Institute on Drug Abuse anticipated a surge in new cases of chemical dependency after the terrorist attacks on the World Trade towers in 2001. In an effort to keep survivors from turning to chemicals, it sponsored a number of counseling services in New York

City. However, even with this help, substance abuse centers throughout the country reported a significant increase in people seeking treatment.

A survivor of the World Trade Center attacks explains: "I was in the first tower. I barely got out before it fell. It was much worse than anyone could ever imagine. It haunts me. When I close my eyes I can still hear the whooshing sound and taste the ashes. It's as if I'm there all over again. I never drank, but now I find myself drinking quite a bit. It's the only way I can blot out the memories."[19]

Experts witnessed a similar trend after the 1995 bombing in Oklahoma City. Former U.S. Department of Health, Education, and Welfare secretary Joseph Califano Jr. maintains, "I think we are talking about an epidemic of self-medication for post-traumatic stress sparked by terrorism. The demand for drugs and alcohol treatment will continue to rise as people absorb the events and come to grips with ongoing threats."[20]

Seeking a competitive edge

While some people abuse chemicals to deal with emotional issues, other people become dependent upon chemicals in an effort to gain a competitive edge. This is especially true in the case of students who often abuse amphetamines in order to cram for exams and finish term papers. However, once the stimulating effect of the drug leaves their bodies, these students start to crash, becoming so tired that they are unable to function normally. To counteract this effect, these students frequently take more amphetamines in order to stay alert. This becomes a dangerous cycle that ends in chemical dependency.

Many professional bodybuilders also seek to gain a competitive edge by abusing chemicals. Because competitive bodybuilders are judged on muscularity and lack of body fat, they frequently combine anabolic steroids that increase their muscularity with amphetamines, which lessen their appetite causing them to lose body fat. Although the combination of these drugs may indeed give bodybuilders a competitive edge over other contestants by giving them an outwardly winning physique, inwardly they are harming their bodies.

Enhancing appearance

In a similar fashion, dieters frequently abuse amphetamines in order to enhance their appearance. Because these drugs boost a person's metabolism and depress his or her appetite, doctors sometimes prescribe them for overweight patients. Problems arise when patients attempt to hasten the weight loss process by taking more than the prescribed dosage of amphetamines. Since the body quickly adapts to the effects of amphetamines, this type of abuse rapidly leads to dependence. A woman who was dependent on amphetamines relates, "I was a chunky teenager. My mother took me to the doctor for diet pills when I was sixteen. I took one pill a day. When one pill didn't do the job, I graduated to four or five. The pills were magical in reducing my weight. But I grew up totally whacked out on them. I didn't know it at the time, but I was addicted."[21]

Peer pressure

Even though many people become dependent upon chemicals because of internal pressure, some people abuse chemicals because of pressure from their friends. This type of influence is known as peer pressure.

A teenage girl watches her friends roll a joint. Young people often succumb to peer pressure to try chemicals.

Peer pressure arises in social situations in which a person's friends or acquaintances use drugs and pressure him or her to do likewise. This pressure leads people to feel like they must use chemicals in order to fit into a group.

Although peer pressure influences people of all ages, it is a particular problem for young people who have a strong need to belong. Just how powerful the influence of peer pressure is on teenagers has been shown in a psychological experiment that was conducted in the 1990s at the University of Mississippi. In this experiment a group of college students were shown a picture of two lines in which one line was obviously longer than the other. The students were told that they would be asked, in front of some new group members, which line was longer and they were instructed to answer incorrectly. Then the new members, who had received no instructions, were brought into the group and asked the same question. Even though it was obvious which line was actually longer, the majority of the new members agreed with those who knowingly gave the wrong answer. Later, each of the new members admitted that they knew the correct answer but felt compelled to answer incorrectly in order to fit into the group.

Experts say that this same kind of peer pressure causes many young people to experiment with chemicals even when they know of the dangers. This is because they do not want to feel singled out or become less popular with their peers. Miller Newton, the director of KIDS of North Jersey, a drug treatment program in New Jersey, explains: "As teenagers pull away from their parents, they come to depend on their friends for emotional support and a sense of identity. For many, that means joining the crowd, even if they don't feel comfortable with the crowd's activities—such as drug abuse."[22]

Family behavior

In a similar manner, people can be influenced by members of their family to abuse chemicals. This is especially true when young family members witness respected older family members abusing chemicals. This type of behavior makes chemical abuse seem acceptable to younger, impressionable family members. A number of studies have proven that when parents or older siblings abuse chemicals, younger family members are more likely to abuse chemicals as well. One such study, for example, that was conducted in San Francisco in 1992 shows that teenagers living in households with one smoker are twice as likely to become dependent on tobacco as teenagers in nonsmoking families. A young woman explains how her family members' chemical dependency influenced her:

> My mother was an alcoholic. My pharmacist father used to give her strange things like Elavil [a mood-altering drug] to help her depressive times. It was only years later—like where was I?—that I realized that not everyone had a dish cabinet at home filled with all sorts of mood-altering medicines rather than cups and saucers. It might be said that I did a fair amount of chemical abuse over the years.[23]

Often older family members introduce younger members to chemical abuse. In fact, 19 percent of people in drug treatment programs say that a family member introduced them to drugs. More surprisingly, a 2000 report by Phoenix House, a drug treatment facility in New York, Texas, Florida, and California, indicates that one in five people in drug treatment first took drugs with their parents. According to an article by Adam Marcus for *iMedReview*, an online health news service, "Children have a greater chance of receiving drugs from a family member than from a professional drug dealer. If the parents use drugs with the kids, you increase the probability of the kids using drugs."[24]

The influence of society

Friends and family are not the only external sources influencing people to abuse chemicals. Society also plays a role. This is especially true of the media, which frequently glamorize the use of cigarettes, alcohol, and drugs in movies, music videos, and advertisements. Because the goal of advertisements is to sell a product, when a television commercial, for example, shows a group of happy, good-looking people having fun drinking beer, the message is that drinking beer promotes good times. This makes some people want to imitate that behavior because they believe it will result in similar "good times."

NASCAR racer Sterling Marlin celebrates a victory. Many sporting events are sponsored by the alcohol industry and play a major role in influencing people to abuse chemicals.

Moreover, many sporting events are sponsored by the alcohol industry and famous athletes frequently star in beer commercials. In addition, popular music often has lyrics glamorizing the use of drugs and alcohol, as do scenes in movies and music videos. Athletes, musicians, and actors are powerful role models for many people, and the sight of them abusing chemicals—or even the belief that they do—can strongly influence audiences to do the same.

Whether people are influenced by the media, their family or friends, or by problems inside themselves, when they turn to drugs, alcohol, and tobacco in order to be more glamorous, fit in, or cope with emotional issues the result is chemical dependency.

3

The Effects of Chemical Dependency

WHEN PEOPLE BECOME dependent on chemicals, the harm that the chemicals do is not limited to the user. Because chemical dependency impairs a person's judgment and changes his or her behavior, it negatively impacts the user's family and friends and causes problems for society.

Effects on families and friends

When people become dependent upon chemicals their lives are driven by their need for the chemical. This changes their personalities, making them increasingly self-centered since their main interest in life becomes getting high. As a result, they often avoid old friends who do not abuse chemicals and replace them with new friends who share their main interest—drug abuse. It also causes them to ignore family commitments if these commitments interfere with getting high. A man who missed his brother's wedding because of his cocaine dependency recalls his experience:

My baby brother was getting married, and I was his best man. The night before the wedding was wild. My bud and me scored an eightball [three grams] of premo coke. We tooted it all up and went out and partied till the bars closed. My baby brother was getting married, right? So why not party? I must have done a half dozen shots of tequila. I was soaring, feeling no pain. I woke up the next day around two o'clock. The wedding was at noon. I'd missed it. I didn't care; coke was my life. All I could think about was scoring. When I finally made it over to the church, they were cleaning up. My brother was gone. But my mama was still there, and the look on her face killed me. [25]

Financial problems

Similarly, chemically dependent people often ignore work commitments that interfere with their addiction. They are typically absent from or tardy to work because of drinking or

An alcoholic husband shouts at his family. Chemical abuse affects every aspect of the addict's life.

drug abuse. Experts estimate that absenteeism is three times higher for substance abusers than for other workers. In financial terms, the results of work absenteeism and lost production costs the United States over $60 billion a year, an amount larger than the gross national product of many emerging nations.

Moreover, when chemically dependent people do go to work, impaired judgment caused by chemical abuse results in poor work performance. In many cases substance abusers' poor judgment threatens their safety and that of their coworkers and people in their care, leading to 25 percent of all accidents in the workplace. One particularly disturbing accident in 1991 involved a cocaine-dependent train engineer who crashed a New York City subway train killing seven people and injuring 170 others.

Not surprisingly, the combination of absenteeism and poor work performance results in many chemically dependent people losing their jobs. This affects the financial security of their families. The results can be devastating, causing families to live in poverty and face problems like hunger and homelessness. It is estimated that 38 percent of all homeless Americans are chemically dependent. A young woman whose mother's alcoholism led the family to become homeless attests,

> My mom's a licensed beautician, and she's very good. But when my mom's drinking, she misses quite a bit of work. She'll

Chemical Dependency and the Workplace

- Percentage of workers who have a drug or alcohol problem: 16
- Number of work-related fatalities due to alcohol or drug use: 5,000
- Lost productivity due to alcohol and drug use: $44 billion per year
- As compared to nonusers, alcohol and drug abusers:
  - are late 3 times more than other employees
  - use 3 times more sick days
  - have 4 times as many on-the-job accidents
  - use 8 times as many hospital days

stand up her clients if she's on a binge. Last year, she was fired from the salon she was working in because she missed too many appointments. The other salons didn't want to hire her because of her drinking problem. When our rent was due, we had no money to pay. After a few months, we were evicted. We lived in an abandoned building after that. [26]

A student in a drug-induced high stares at his pencil. Chemical dependency leads many students to drop out of school.

School dropouts

The same factors that cause chemically dependent adults to lose their jobs influence chemically dependent teenagers to drop out of high school. Chemically dependent teenagers often skip school in order to get high. When they are in school, poor judgment often causes them to get in trouble, and impaired thinking causes their grades to fall. As a result, many chemically dependent teenagers drop out. However, people who do not complete high school face severe economic consequences. Dropouts generally have a difficult time finding good, secure, decent-paying jobs, since even many entry-level jobs require a high school diploma. In fact, the unemployment rate for high school dropouts is twice as high as that for high school graduates. In Chicago, for instance, there are six un-employed unskilled workers for every entry-level job.

The financial impact of dropping out is not felt by the dropout alone. Many dropouts become financially dependent on their families for years to come, while others become dependent upon society. It is estimated that 45 percent of all women on welfare, for example, are high school dropouts. A high school teacher explains:

> I've been a teacher for thirty-five years. I've taught two genera-tions of kids from the same families. I've seen hundreds of kids graduate and dozens drop out. Most of the kids who drop out have drug problems. It's common for them to wind up in jail or on welfare. Fifteen years down the line, I wind up teaching their kids. Unfortunately, their kids often grow up living in poverty, dependent on the government for food and housing. In some cases, they all live in the family house and their aging parents are forced to support them all. It's hard on everyone, especially the innocent kids and the grandparents. [27]

Child neglect

In addition to ignoring school, jobs, family obligations, and friends, when people become wrapped up in using drugs or other chemical substances, they often neglect their chil-dren if caring for their children interferes with their chance to get high. Consequently, according to a 1999 study by the Na-tional Center on Addiction and Substance Abuse at Columbia University, children whose parents abuse chemicals are more than four times likelier to be neglected than children of par-ents who do not abuse chemicals. Moreover, nearly 90 per-cent of these children are placed in foster care. A daughter of an alcoholic describes her experience:

> I love my mom. She's the best. It hurts that I can't live with her. Right now I live with my grandma because my mom isn't able to take care of me. She has a drinking problem. It's hard when she's drinking. She isn't herself then. I have to take care of both of us. I try, but I'm thirteen. She's tried to quit, but she's not strong enough. Last year she quit, and I got to live with her. But she started up again. When Child Protective Services found out, they sent me back to live at my grandma's. I know it's for the best, and I love my grandma. But it hurts. I miss my mom. [28]

Domestic violence

Neglect is not the only effect of chemical dependency on families. Chemicals such as alcohol, stimulants, inhalants, and anabolic steroids, which cause anger and violent behavior, often cause people who abuse them to commit acts of domestic violence. Nationwide, 75 percent of all spousal-abuse victims report that their abuser was under the influence of chemicals. A woman who was abused by her alcoholic husband recalls, "For twelve years my husband drank himself blind every weekend, and for twelve years he physically abused me every weekend." [29]

Even more troubling, the Child Welfare Protection League of America reports that parental abuse of drugs or alcohol is the most common reason for child abuse. According to a

A little girl cowers as her father berates her. Chemically dependent parents are very likely to abuse their children.

Columbia University report, substance abuse is at the root of seven out of ten cases of child abuse. Moreover, children of chemically dependent parents are three times more likely to be abused than children of nonusers.

Suicide

Besides physically injuring family members, many chemically dependent people try to injure themselves. Depression and frustration over financial problems coupled with impaired judgment caused by substance abuse are linked to suicide. Approximately thirty thousand people in the United States commit suicide each year. Eleven thousand have a history of chemical dependency. These numbers do not include an additional thirty-three thousand chemically dependent people who attempt suicide and fail, but not without injuring themselves first.

Suicide affects not only the victim. It is estimated that every suicide impacts at least ten other people. These people include the victim's family, friends, coworkers, and peers. Moreover, the effect is long-lasting. Like all deaths, suicide leaves loved ones grieving. However, because suicide victims take their own lives, loved ones often experience feelings of guilt, anger, and rejection. They frequently wonder if they could have done something to prevent the suicide. According to an Internet article on grief and suicide, "The person who commits suicide sentences the survivors to deal with many negative feelings, and more, to become obsessed with thoughts regarding their own actual or possible role in having precipitated the suicidal act or having failed to abort or prevent it. It is a heavy load."[30]

Dealing with suicide often makes it difficult for loved ones to resume their normal lives. Work and school often suffer. Many survivors develop severe depression, and some even attempt to take their own lives. It is estimated that people who are bereaved by suicide are six times more likely to attempt suicide than other people. In addition, when the suicide victim is the primary breadwinner, families often experience financial problems as a result of the person's death. A man whose chemically dependent father committed suicide talks about the effect on his family:

> I was fourteen when my father, who was an alcoholic, committed suicide. It took a long time for my family to spring back, and

to be honest, I don't believe we ever have. My mother slipped into a cycle of depression and tranquilizer abuse that lasted until she died. It was especially hard for my sister and me. Our whole lives changed. Money was tight. Our mother was never the same, and we were forced to become adults long before we were ready. Even today, forty years later, I don't understand how my father could have left his family. I still feel rejected. I have two children of my own. I'd do anything for them. Obviously, my father cared more about himself than his family. I'll never forgive him for that. [31]

Inmates at the Iowa Correctional Institution for Women take part in group therapy. More than 80 percent of the U.S. prison population has a history of substance abuse.

Effects on society

Families, friends, coworkers, and peers are not the only people who are negatively impacted by chemical dependency. Chemical dependency has a far-reaching effect on society. The combination of impaired judgment, the compulsion to abuse chemicals, financial problems, anger, and violent behavior leads many chemically dependent people to commit crimes that affect many innocent people. The most common of these crimes are stealing and prostitution because substance abusers need to get money to support their dependency. Other crimes associated with substance abuse include rape and homicide. National research indicates that 50 percent of all burglaries, rapes, and homicides are committed by people under the influence of drugs or alcohol. What is more, over 80 percent of the total prison population in the United States, a total of more than 1.7 million people, have a history of substance abuse. These prisoners total more than the individual populations of twelve of the fifty states, and they cost the government, and thus individual taxpayers, more than $3 billion a year. According to the National Center on Addiction and Substance Abuse at Columbia University, "Substance abuse and addiction have fundamentally changed the nature of America's prison population. State and federal prisons and local jails are bursting at the bars with alcohol and drug abusers and addicts. In America, crime and alcohol and drug abuse are joined at the hip."[32]

Unplanned sex

Just as impaired judgment can lead people to commit crimes, it can also increase the probability of people partici-

An obstetrician checks the heartbeat of a premature baby. Abusing chemicals while pregnant can lead to babies born with deformities, brain damage, or drug addiction.

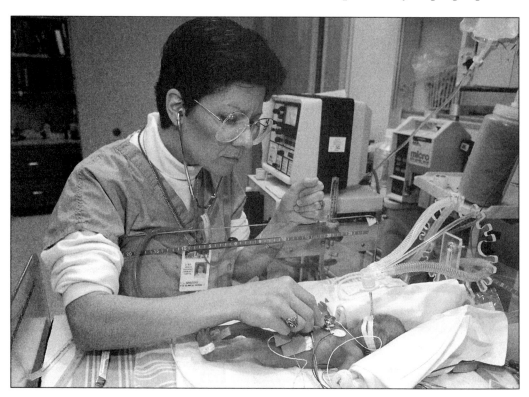

pating in activities they would normally avoid, such as unplanned sex. This puts people at risk of contracting sexually transmitted diseases such as HIV, as well as causing unintended pregnancies. According to a 2002 survey conducted by the Kaiser Family Foundation, 36 percent of the people surveyed reported that drinking or drug use influenced their decisions about sex and 23 percent reported having unprotected sex while abusing chemicals. A former cocaine user admits,

> I know guys like to brag, but not me. My mama raised me to be a
> gentleman. Besides, my sexual exploits aren't anything to brag
> about. When I was doing coke, I fell into bed with any lady who'd
> have me. Most of them were just as coked up as me. Who else
> would've had me? Half the time, I didn't even know the lady's
> name. Who cared? We were just having fun, right? I doubt I ever
> used protection. I was way too high to think about it. All I can say
> is I must have an angel watching out for me. It's a wonder I'm not
> dead of AIDS or the daddy of seven kids. [33]

Effects on the unborn baby

Whether unplanned or planned, once a chemically dependent woman becomes pregnant, chemicals that enter her bloodstream are passed to her fetus through the placenta. Exposure to these chemicals presents a serious health hazard for the fetus. Some chemicals such as alcohol interfere with the fetus's ability to receive sufficient oxygen and nutrition. This can cause skeletal, facial, and organ deformities and stunt or otherwise negatively affect the growth of brain cells. The results include missing fingers and toes, limited movement of joints, crossed eyes, heart and kidney defects, mental retardation, and learning disabilities. These babies are said to have fetal alcohol syndrome. Experts estimate that out of every one thousand babies born in the United States each year thirty-three suffer from fetal alcohol syndrome.

Other drugs such as heroin, cocaine, and crack are known to cause hemorrhaging, or bleeding, in the brains of fetuses exposed to them. This can lead to these babies suffering from impaired motor skills, delayed language development, attention deficit disorder, learning disabilities, and aggressive behavior. According to obstetrician Freeman Miller, "The use of cocaine or crack by the expectant mother is associated with blood vessel complications . . . and is becoming more prevalent as a cause of brain damage in infants."[34]

In addition, fetuses exposed to heroin, amphetamines, cocaine, or tranquilizers are often born addicted to these drugs. Approximately four hundred thousand addicted babies are born in the United States each year, all of whom experience painful withdrawal symptoms. These symptoms include seizures, vomiting, diarrhea, sleep and feeding problems, breathing problems, and hyperactivity. In addition, infants going through drug withdrawal are more prone to respiratory distress, which can lead to death.

As infants exposed to drugs and alcohol grow, they may be so impaired that they require a lifetime of special care including special social, health, psychological, and educational services. According to an Internet report on drug-addicted babies,

> Teachers and administrators report increasing numbers of children who lack social skills and have difficulty keeping pace with routine demands. Some children are persistently withdrawn; others are prone to sudden episodes of violence. Educators have begun attributing these behaviors, as well as a wide range of other behaviors and developmental delays, to the effects of prenatal drug exposure.[35]

Accidents

Since impaired judgment hinders people's ability to think clearly, substance abuse may also make people feel able to function normally despite being high. In this manner, some people under the influence of chemicals take to the roads believing they can safely operate a motor vehicle. But feelings of drowsiness, anxiety, excitement, overconfidence, and altered perception all cause reckless driving. A 1997 study at the Maryland Shock and Trauma Center in Baltimore found that over half the accident victims treated at the center were chemically dependent upon drugs or alcohol.

Chemical users are not the only people affected; so are people in vehicles they collide with and those people's families and friends. The annual economic cost of substance-related accidents is more than $114 billion per year. In 2001 more than thirty-five thousand people in the United States were killed in drug or alcohol-related car accidents, a number

Soldiers assess the damage done to a Cadillac involved in a drunk-driving incident. The impaired judgment and reckless driving of chemical users cause thousands of deaths each year.

that translates to about forty-eight people a day. At the same time, more than five hundred thousand people were injured in these types of accidents. A typical case is that of a Texas family who were driving home from Thanksgiving dinner in 2000 when their car was struck by a drunk driver, killing four family members and severely injuring three others.

Insurance experts estimate that at the current rate, one-third of all Americans will be involved in a substance-related accident at some time in their lives. A woman who crashed her car three times in one month while under the influence of depressants, seriously injuring others each time, explains: "I will always know in my heart that I could have killed those people. It doesn't matter that I didn't kill them; it matters that I could have."[36]

Although chemical dependency does not always lead to death or tragedy, the potential is ever present. The medical risks to the abuser and the risks of injury to others are increased when chemical dependency is an issue. Whether by causing accidents or hurting innocent people, unborn babies, families, coworkers, or friends, it is clear that when a person abuses chemicals the impact is far-reaching.

4

Treatment

SINCE CHEMICAL DEPENDENCY impacts substance abusers' families, friends, and society, many chemically dependent people undergo treatment not because they want to end their substance abuse but rather because their loved ones or the law requires it. Unfortunately, studies show that people who are forced into treatment do not do as well as those who seek treatment voluntarily. In fact, only about 20 percent of people forced into treatment stop abusing chemicals after being released from treatment, whereas about 50 percent of people who willingly seek treatment remain chemical free. Experts say the reason is that since substance abuse is deliberate, treatment is most effective when people want to stop using chemicals. Addiction expert Elizabeth Connell Henderson explains, "It is important to remember that there is an element of will involved in addiction. If you are willing, if you remain open to suggestions, you can make it." [37]

Admitting the problem

The first step in effectively ending chemical dependency occurs when substance abusers admit that they have a problem. Although this sounds simple, many chemically dependent people are unable or unwilling to do this. They enjoy the effects of substance abuse so much that they ignore the negative consequences. This is known as denial. A former alcoholic relates,

> Of all the things I've learned about addictive behavior, denial is still the most perplexing. I seemed to have an amazing ability to stare right at things and not know what I was looking at. For

An inmate discusses his chemical dependency with a counselor. Treatment is most effective when substance abusers seek it of their own volition.

twenty-five years I denied my abuse of alcohol. I didn't just refuse to admit it. I absolutely, positively, one-hundred percent didn't think I was anything other than a "social drinker." Never mind routine drunk driving, waking up in a neighbor's lawn or an unfamiliar bed, black-outs, depression, rage and abusiveness. I really couldn't see the problem.[38]

Intervention

Clearly, denial stands in the way of chemically dependent individuals seeking treatment. Therefore, in order to convince substance abusers that they need help, an intervention may be held. One man explains why he is organizing an intervention for a family member: "A person in my family is drinking too much. I worry he will have an accident and die. I want him to stop drinking so he will be happy and the rest of us can stop worrying. Nothing we have done so far has done any good. An intervention is our last hope."[39]

During an intervention concerned friends and family members respectfully confront a substance abuser with the consequences of his or her addiction. The relatives and friends present facts about how the person's chemical dependency has adversely affected the substance abuser and his or her loved ones. Such a presentation often exposes feelings of anger, sadness, and guilt. Since this can be emotionally difficult for the abuser and the family, interventions are often conducted by substance abuse professionals. According to one such professional at the Intervention Center of Virginia, "No one can predict with certainty how someone will react. Acceptance, anger, hope, confusion are all usually present to some degree, and sooner, or later will emerge."[40]

Generally the mounting evidence presented during the intervention helps the addict admit there is a problem. At this point, different treatment options are presented. According to substance abuse treatment experts at Spencer Recovery Centers in Laguna Beach, California, "The process of intervention is designed to smash through the dependent's rigid denial defense mechanisms and break through to reality. Intervention is ninety to ninety-five percent successful in confronting, with love and compassion, the drug dependent individual."[41]

Experiencing a crisis

In some cases an intervention does not help, or it is not held before chemically dependent people experience a critical life-changing event caused by their substance abuse. Such an event, or crisis, often convinces substance abusers that

---

Substance Abuse Treatment Facts

There were 1.9 million admissions in 1995 to publicly funded substance abuse treatment centers:
- 54 percent were for alcohol abuse; 46 percent were for illicit drug abuse treatment.
- 70 percent were male; 30 percent were female.
- 56 percent were white, followed by African Americans (26 percent), Hispanics (7.7 percent), Native Americans (2.2 percent), and Asians and Pacific Islanders (0.6 percent).
- The largest number of illicit drug treatment admissions were for cocaine (38.3 percent), followed by heroin (25.5 percent), and marijuana (19.1 percent).

they have a problem, leading them to seek treatment. Each person's crisis is different. In some cases it can be minor, such as losing a promotion at work. In other cases it may be a more serious crisis such as an automobile accident, being arrested, losing a job or important relationship, or losing a child to foster care. The dependent person may also suffer from a health problem such as liver failure due to substance abuse. Such an event is often a low point in an addict's life, and is commonly called "hitting bottom."

Experts agree that no matter what event causes an addict to hit bottom, the event results in the addict realizing that the consequences of chemical abuse outweigh the benefits. "I literally was on my knees puking and drinking Smirnoff 160 [vodka] at the same time," one former alcoholic and drug abuser recalls. "What happened to me was the booze turned on me—my liver stopped functioning. Unfiltered alcohol flooded my bloodstream in all its toxic mayhem. The only things I knew a lot about were death and alcoholism. From there, the only direction was up." [42]

A recovering crack addict is reunited with her children after joining a drug treatment program. Losing a child to foster care can shock a person into seeking treatment.

Seeking treatment

Once a person accepts that he or she has a problem, there are a number of different treatment options available. These include residential treatment, outpatient treatment, and twelve-step programs. Although these treatments utilize different approaches, they all share the same goal of helping patients to become sober while making them aware of their problem. In this manner, patients gain the tools to remain drug and alcohol free upon their release.

Detoxification

No matter what form of treatment is used, all treatment begins with detoxification. Detoxification, or "detox," involves cleansing the body of the damaging effects of alcohol or drugs. In order to do this, patients must abstain from using the chemical they are dependent upon. Because chemically dependent people's brains crave the substance they are addicted to, detoxification can be both physically and emotionally difficult. Often the body reacts with physical and psychological effects known as withdrawal symptoms.

Withdrawal symptoms can range from mildly uncomfortable to severe depending on what chemical the person is addicted to, and how long and how often it has been used. Depending on the chemical, withdrawal symptoms may include hallucinations, nausea, vomiting, anxiety, sweating, body aches, muscle cramps and spasms, fever, insomnia, loss of appetite, and seizures.

Because withdrawal symptoms such as seizures and hallucinations can be dangerous, many people weather detox in a hospital or drug treatment center, while others detoxify at home with the help of loved ones and frequent doctor visits. Fortunately, withdrawal symptoms disappear once the chemical clears the body. The rate at which this occurs depends on the chemical. For instance, alcohol clears the body in about five days, whereas other chemicals, like depressants, can take months to clear the body.

Residential treatment

Once chemically dependent people have gone through detoxification, they need treatment in order to learn how to resist the temptation to start using again. They also must learn how to make the transition from life as an addict to living soberly.

Many chemically dependent people receive residential treatment. This is especially true for individuals addicted to chemicals such as cocaine or heroin that have a strong physical and emotional hold on users and, thus, are hardest to stop using. Just as the name implies, residential treatment involves substance abusers living in a treatment facility twenty-four hours a day for anywhere from one month to two years.

Each residential treatment center is different. Some are as luxurious as a fine hotel. Others have a boot camp atmosphere with strict rules that include prescribed "lights out" and wake-up times. Such facilities might also ban smoking, drinking caffeine, or using makeup, and the most restrictive centers will securely lock down the entrances and exits to prohibit patients from leaving before treatment is complete. However, all residential treatment facilities provide round-the-clock care for patients in a caring, stable environment.

Generally each patient's treatment is tailored to meet his or her individual needs. It is based on the addict's age, gender, severity of addiction, and specific chemicals abused, as well as the addict's attitude, former behavior, and physical and emotional state. However, no matter what the patient's individual treatment plan is, treatment services are structured with prescribed activities geared toward helping the patient to recover. Treatment services commonly include medical consultations with doctors and nurses, individual and group therapy, and peer discussion sessions conducted by psychologists and certified addiction counselors. These sessions are aimed at helping patients eliminate any remaining feelings of denial and discover and deal with the reasons that they abuse chemicals. In addition, most residential treatment facilities reeducate patients, teaching them how to cope with their problems in order to avoid turning to chemicals as a solution upon their release from the treatment center.

Often residential treatment addiction counselors are recovered substance abusers themselves who, through firsthand experience, understand what the patients are experiencing.

Having lived through addiction, they are able to both mentor and confront the patients when necessary. This provides patients with a balance of compassionate care and tough love. According to addiction counselors at Serenity Lane Alcohol and Drug Treatment Centers located throughout Oregon,

> It's important to remember that addiction to alcohol and other drugs is life-threatening and thrives on denial. Alcoholic/addicts often demonstrate thinking errors, self-centeredness, and immaturity. Each of these must be addressed as compassionately as possible and as directly as necessary. That means the counselor must break down this structure to change the person's life. I'm more interested in saving your [the patient's] life than sparing your feelings. [43]

Although residential treatment can be difficult, the results are often worth the effort. About 50 percent of all people who enter residential treatment permanently recover from chemical dependency. "It was harsh," one patient affirms. "I was really hurting. I was totally powerless. But I was messed up.

Patients at a residential treatment facility prepare a meal. Treatment facilities give chemically dependent people the tools they need to make the transition to sober living.

56

Now, I think of AARC [Alberta Adolescent Recovery Center, a residential treatment center in Alberta, Canada] as my birthplace. It is where I got a new beginning."[44]

Outpatient treatment

For patients who do not have the time to commit to residential treatment, outpatient treatment offers another way to break the bonds of chemical dependency. Similar to residential treatment in the services offered and in that it is structured to each individual's needs, outpatient treatment allows patients to live at home while receiving treatment. It does not require patients to take time off from work or school, or leave their families. Instead, people in outpatient treatment are re-

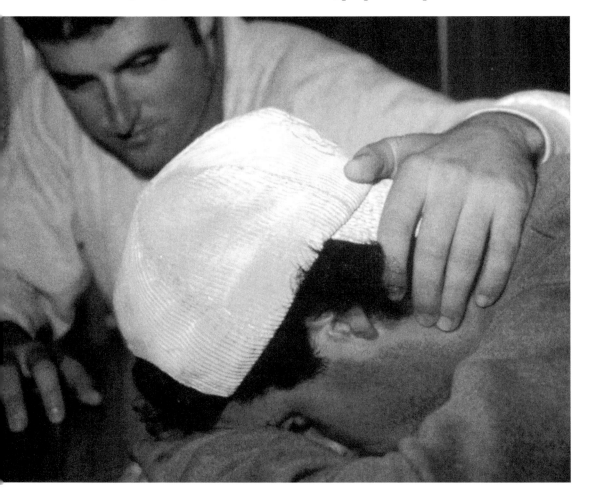

A counselor comforts his patient. Both residential and outpatient treatment require patients to attend group therapy sessions and see counselors regularly.

quired to attend group therapy and peer discussion sessions in a hospital or addiction treatment center about four nights per week. In addition, each patient is usually assigned to a counselor who helps the patient master the skills needed to remain drug and alcohol free upon release. Since a person in outpatient treatment usually lives at home, his or her family members are required to attend separate counseling groups where they learn how they can best support the patient's recovery.

Outpatient treatment usually lasts from four to six weeks. It is most effective for people who are eager to stop abusing, are at an early stage of addiction, or are addicted to less powerful chemicals such as alcohol or marijuana. This is because patients receiving outpatient treatment face more temptation to abuse chemicals than those in the restricted environment of residential treatment. Consequently, patients with severe addictions and those who are ambivalent about quitting often do not have the willpower necessary to resist substance abuse when faced with the challenge. As a result only about 30 percent of the people who receive outpatient treatment permanently recover from chemical dependency. Author and addiction expert Al J. Mooney explains,

> For some people outpatient programs can be risky. Dredging up deep feeling can lead to dropping into a bar after a session, or to dropping out of the program entirely. At an inpatient [residential] program, it's not easy to pick up and leave. And there is time to give those feelings a decent burial before you are sent out into the world. But for those who can benefit from it [outpatient treatment], there is the advantage of learning to stay sober in the real world rather than in the sheltered world of an inpatient facility.[45]

The advantages of outpatient treatment, however, are entirely dependent upon the commitment of the individual. The patient, who will have to willingly attend counseling sessions and seminars, has to accept that much of his or her new life will be devoted to treatment. A patient who recovered as a result of outpatient treatment describes his experience:

> I have no memories more pure or important than those of my outpatient treatment sessions. There I began a process of learning about alcohol, addiction, feelings, fellowship, belonging,

support, love, gentleness, responsibility, and about who I really am. I learned things about life I'd never known. It [treatment] was a series of classes on chemical dependency, addictive behavior, and personal change. Sounds like a lot, doesn't it? It is. It's a whole new life.[46]

Twelve-step programs

As a supplement to outpatient treatment, many people take part in a twelve-step program such as Alcoholics Anonymous, Narcotics Anonymous, or Cocaine Anonymous. Other people recover solely through a twelve-step program. Like support groups, twelve-step programs involve a group of people with the same problem who meet regularly to discuss their addiction, share their common experiences, and give each other support and understanding in an effort to assist each other in recovery. A former alcoholic and drug addict who attributes her recovery to Narcotics Anonymous describes how the group helped her:

> I walked into the doors of a room and found people who didn't ask me why do you do that [abuse drugs]? They all knew why and they loved me still. All they cared about was what I wanted to do about my problem and how they could help. How wonderful it was to find out that I wasn't alone, wasn't judged, and wasn't going to live without hope anymore. Today I can smile again, and I can share that with others.[47]

In addition, like in most support groups, twelve-step group meetings are led by members rather than professional counselors. However, unlike the structure of other support groups, twelve-step programs are based on twelve specific steps, the basic premise of which is that members must admit that they are powerless against alcohol or drugs and that their lives have become unmanageable. With the help of individual sponsors and role models whom they select from the group, members are expected to systematically work through each step in order to recover from their addiction. Like addiction counselors in residential treatment centers, twelve-step sponsors are usually further along in their own recovery and, thus, understand what new members are going through. And, because they are not close friends or family members, sponsors have only one main interest in their sponsoree's life—to keep that individual from abusing chemicals. Consequently, sponsors are objectively supporting the sponsorees' triumphs on the road to recovery, while at the same time pointing out their failures. A twelve-step-program member talks about his sponsor: "I picked somebody who had what I wanted, who lived the kind of life I wanted. Somebody who would not tell me what I wanted to hear, but what I needed to hear. I needed somebody to be hard on me, but who could also love me when I was down on myself."[48]

In order to help people resist abusing chemicals, sponsors are available twenty-four hours a day. They can be called whenever an individual feels tempted to abuse chemicals. This provides addicts a lifeline against temptation. A patient recalls, "The first time I called my sponsor in the middle of the night, he came right over to my house and sat with me and we talked and talked. And I got through the night."[49]

There is no time limit on how long people attend twelve-step programs. Since the temptation to abuse chemicals can plague former addicts for most of their lives, twelve-step-program membership is ongoing. At first people may attend meetings every day, then as their recovery progresses, people attend meetings whenever they feel it is necessary. In order to reward people who remain sober, most twelve-step groups give members pins or medallions recognizing their length of sobriety. This is done in a special ceremony before the group. For example, a recovering cocaine addict who has not abused cocaine for a year is honored with a one-year pin commemorating his or her abstinence. It is thought that being recognized in this manner helps motivate addicts to resist substance abuse.

Since twelve-step programs are anonymous, there are no statistics available about their success rates. Nevertheless, it is estimated that about 40 percent of all people in twelve-step programs permanently recover.

It is clear that recovering from chemical dependency is difficult. Withdrawal can be painful, and treatment is time consuming and arduous. In order to be most successful, it requires a strong commitment by the patient who wants to be cured. However, when treatment is successful, addicts and substance abuse professionals agree the results are well worth the effort. A former cocaine addict explains,

> Before treatment, coke [cocaine] was my life. Nothing else mattered. I thought I was living, but I could have been dead for all the good I was doing. Treatment was rough. I had to look at myself good and hard. That wasn't easy. I hated myself. I hated my life. I hated what I'd become. Treatment turned me around. I'm 100 percent changed. I've got my life back. Life's still a struggle. Whose life isn't? But nothing could make me use coke again. Treatment did that for me, and that, my friend, is a miracle.[50]

5

Staying Chemical Free

SINCE THE BRAIN retains memories of pleasurable feelings, even after people have successfully completed treatment they often retain the desire to abuse chemicals. When former substance abusers submit to this desire and abuse chemicals only one time, they are said to have slipped up. When the abuse continues, they are said to have experienced a relapse. Approximately 50 percent of all chemically dependent people relapse at least once after going through treatment, and it is not uncommon for addicts to experience five relapses before recovering completely. Experts say that relapses are often triggered by a number of psychological and visual cues that remind the brain of the pleasurable sensations of substance abuse, reactivating an urge for drugs or alcohol. These cues vary from person to person, but generally include contact with drugs or alcohol, or with people, activities, and feelings that encouraged the person to abuse chemicals in the past. Therefore, in order to avoid a relapse, people must avoid these triggers. This involves making a number of changes in their lives.

Avoiding old friends

Because socializing with drinking and drug-abusing friends can trigger the desire for these substances in recovering addicts, these people must be avoided in order to avoid a relapse. Such old friends, whose lifestyle is often centered on substance abuse, may tempt recovering addicts with readily

61

Recovering addicts avoid social gatherings where chemicals are available. Being around friends who drink or use drugs can lead to a relapse.

available chemicals. Consequently, substance abuse professionals and recovering addicts agree that avoiding these people is necessary. A recovering addict recalls,

> When I got out of treatment, I thought it would be okay to hang with my old coke buddies just like always. They were my buds, right? But all they talked about was getting high. I didn't think talk could bother me. It was just words, right? But just the talk had me salivating like a dog. Watching them tooting up [snorting cocaine] was torture. I knew if I didn't run for my life I'd crash and burn. There was no way I could hang with them and stay clean. [51]

In an effort to solve this problem, instead of socializing with substance-abusing friends, many recovering addicts renew old friendships with people who do not drink or abuse drugs. These friendships are often with friends whom substance abusers may have stopped seeing when they started abusing chemicals. Others build new friendships with people they meet in treatment programs who share similar interests and a desire to avoid substance abuse. A young man explains, "Once I realized that I couldn't hang with my old coke buds, I started hanging with a couple of guys from Cocaine Anonymous. They're good guys, there for me when I need them and, believe it or not, we can party together without getting high."[52]

Avoiding social events

Just as associating with substance-abusing friends can tempt a recovering addict to abuse chemicals, so can attending social events where chemicals are available. Consequently, many former substance abusers change the type of social activities they participate in, in order to prevent a relapse. Many avoid going to bars, restaurants, parties, or raves, for example, where they know alcohol or drugs are available. "For me any place I used to drink is immediate death," a former alcoholic relates. "A smoke-filled bar, an easy comfortable atmosphere and a nice looking lady—no way I can stay dry. So I stay away."[53]

Instead, formerly chemically dependent people attend social activities where chemicals are not readily obtainable. Such activities often include family gatherings or church-sponsored events. Furthermore, when patients must attend events where alcohol is served, many recovering addicts take a friend from their twelve-step program or a supportive family member with them to help them resist temptation. Addiction expert Al J. Mooney advises, "Just as swimmers shouldn't swim in deep water without a buddy, it's best for alcoholics/addicts in recovery not to circulate alone. Whether it's a sister's wedding, a grandmother's birthday party or just a walk that will take you past your old happy hunting grounds—bar, liquor store, drug corner—you should try to avoid doing it solo."[54]

Avoiding feelings that led to chemical dependency

Avoiding substance-abusing people and social events where chemicals are available can be difficult. It is even harder, however, for former addicts to avoid emotional issues that led them to become dependent on chemicals. Therefore, in order to avoid a relapse, recovering substance abusers must identify the feelings and emotional issues that caused them to abuse chemicals and try to deal with them. Counseling and group therapy sessions conducted during treatment help patients begin this process. However, many people find that seeing a psychologist once treatment is over helps them to deal effectively with issues such as low self-esteem, depression, and thrill-seeking behavior. Discussing these issues with a psychologist helps individuals become more self-aware. With increased self-awareness former substance abusers can identify the causes of their negative emotions, then explore ways to change or avoid these feelings and, thus, avoid relapse. A woman who was addicted to amphetamines explains how visiting a psychologist helped her:

A young woman meets with her psychologist. Discussing issues that contribute to substance abuse are integral to remaining chemical free.

My problem wasn't only that I was addicted to diet pills, but why I was addicted. Until I dealt with my poor self-image, I was on a merry-go-round of addiction and treatment. Once I started seeing a psychologist I learned to accept myself for the big beautiful woman I am. Once I accepted myself, my problem was solved. I no longer needed pills to make me feel good about the way I looked. [55]

Handling stress

The combination of confronting emotional issues, avoiding substance-abusing friends and situations, and coping with daily life without drugs or alcohol puts many former substance abusers under a great deal of stress. Since many people originally start abusing chemicals in order to cope with stress, it is important that former addicts learn how to handle stress in order to avoid a relapse. In fact, a number of studies indicate that stress is the number one cause of chemical dependency relapse. One 1999 National Institutes of Health study, for example, found that when former cocaine abusers were exposed to personal stress, they reported significant increases in their craving for cocaine. Scientists think that addiction to cocaine and opiates, in particular, permanently lowers the brain's ability to produce cortisol, a chemical that helps the body deal with stress. Therefore, former addicts have less natural ability to deal with stress than people whose brains produce normal amounts of cortisol and, thus, are more likely to turn to chemicals to help them cope.

Aromatherapy

One way some former substance abusers deal with stress is aromatherapy. Aromatherapy is based on the theory that the sense of smell influences physical and psychological reactions. Consequently, it uses scent to improve mental and physical health and well-being.

In aromatherapy, people inhale warmed essential oils derived from plants that are believed to have tranquilizing and stress-relieving properties. Such oils include lavender, vanilla, lemon balm, jasmine, and chamomile. People report that inhaling these oils makes them feel more relaxed and less troubled by stress. The oil is usually placed in a special electric diffuser or an aroma lamp. There, it is heated up and dispersed into the air as a mist. The mist acts as a relaxant and calms the patient. "I have a lot of trouble dealing with stress," a former abuser of tranquilizers explains.

> It [stress] was the reason I started popping pills. I know myself.
> I know that stress is the only thing that can make me start using
> again. If I want to stay off pills, I have to protect myself from
> stress. Aromatherapy is one of my weapons. I have a diffuser in
> my bedroom, another beside the bathtub, and one in my cubicle
> at work filled with lavender. I wear lavender-based perfume and
> body lotion. I light lavender-scented candles all over my house.
> The scent completely calms me. All I have to do is inhale and I
> feel my heart rate slowing and my body relaxing. I don't need
> pills, I have lavender. [56]

Meditation

Like aromatherapy, meditation is another tool that many former substance abusers find effective in relieving stress and preventing a relapse. While meditating, people use concentration techniques such as silently repeating a word or a chant to clear the mind in order to relax the body and relieve stress. Research has shown that during meditation cortisol levels increase, while other chemicals that raise the body's stress levels, such as adrenaline, decrease. Moreover, when meditation is practiced often, these chemicals remain at optimum levels. As a result, high levels of stress and anxiety that can trigger a craving for drugs or alcohol are reduced.

Although experts are unsure why meditation can change chemical levels in the body, the results of a number of studies are so impressive that many substance abuse experts and former addicts endorse using meditation as a way to reduce stress and prevent a relapse. For example, a twenty-two-month-long study in India in 1994 reported in the *Alcoholism and Treatment Quarterly* compared the relapse rate of ninety-nine recovering substance abusers who practiced a form of meditation known as transcendental meditation to ninety-nine recovering substance abusers who did not. The study found that only 35 percent of the subjects who meditated relapsed, in comparison to 75 percent of the nonmeditators. According to experts writing for the *Addiction Recovery*

Guide, an Internet guide to recovery, "The long-term positive effects of TM [transcendental meditation] seem to be correlated with a reduced relapse rate. TM may not only reduce tension and anxiety, but also enhance a sense of control in anxiety-provoking situations that strengthens the long-term resistance to stress."[57]

Women sit in calm meditation. Meditation is an effective tool in reducing stress and can help substance abusers deal with life without resorting to chemicals.

Tai chi chuan

Combining meditation with physical activity in a practice known as tai chi chuan is another way that many former substance abusers deal with stress. Often referred to as meditation in action, tai chi chuan, also called tai chi, was developed in ancient China as a way to improve mental and physical health by increasing the flow of energy through the body. Tai chi combines physical exercise with mental techniques similar to those used in meditation to relax exercisers and lower stress. Tai chi promotes relaxation and relieves stress by using the whole body in a series of controlled movements that improve balance and strengthen the muscles while controlling breathing and inner thoughts. For this reason tai chi is often used in China to help recovering substance abusers cope with stress and avoid a relapse. In fact, a number of scientific studies conducted in China and reviewed by the U.S. National Institute of Health have shown that daily practice of tai chi lowers blood pressure, which is important in lowering stress levels.

An instructor leads her tai chi class. Used in China to help recovering substance abusers, this ancient Chinese practice balances energy and alleviates stress.

Staying active

Like tai chi, exercise of all kinds is another way recovering addicts relieve stress. Exercise causes the brain to release endorphins, natural chemicals which give the exerciser a feeling of wellness that reduces stress, anxiety, and depression. Moreover, since endorphin levels remain high even when people stop exercising, exercisers are better able to handle stressful situations than nonexercisers. What is more, exercise enhances individuals' physical appearance, which raises their self-esteem, builds strong muscles weakened by substance abuse, increases stamina, and improves overall fitness without the use of chemicals. And, regular exercise leaves little room in a person's schedule for the use of alcohol and drugs.

Although any form of exercise helps relieve stress, yoga, in particular, has been found to be especially effective in helping recovering substance abusers relieve stress and avoid a relapse. Yoga is a form of exercise that originated in ancient India. It involves slow, controlled stretching while the body is held in certain postures. The combination of stretching and posture work relaxes the body and loosens up muscles in the neck, back, and chest that have become stiff and tight as a result of stress. In addition, because holding yoga postures requires strength, control, and concentration, it physically strengthens the weakened bodies of former substance abusers. At the same time it clears the mind. Moreover, the control and persistence required in yoga gives practitioners more confidence in themselves and in their ability to overcome drug cravings. According to addiction psychotherapist Margaret Frederick, "Yoga treats the biology and the psychology of an addict [both current and recovering substance abusers]. Addicts are profoundly out of control internally. They have knee-jerk reactions. The will and determination yoga requires helps people regain control over their body and their mind."[58]

In fact, because yoga is so effective in relieving stress and helping recovering substance abusers resist chemicals, it is commonly used in substance abuse treatment and aftercare programs throughout India. A 1998 study by the United Nations Office on Drugs and Crime looked at one such program at the Nav-Chetna Drug De-addiction and Rehabilitation

Center in Varanasi, India. The study found that former substance abusers who practiced yoga daily were more relaxed and energized, had more self-confidence, and were more able to confront unsolved problems and handle stress than former substance abusers who did not practice yoga. Moreover, approximately 90 percent of the subjects who practiced yoga daily abstained from abusing drugs or alcohol for a period of twenty years. As a result, K. Sharma, director of the center, concluded, "The principal aim of yoga is to help a person overcome physical discomfort and emotional tensions by training her or him to forget unpleasant experiences and to face stressful situations boldly. Yoga offers the promotion of positive health and the protection against stressful events. Thus, the danger of relapse naturally decreases with yoga therapy." [59]

Aerobic exercise

For recovering substance abusers who prefer faster-paced forms of exercise than yoga, scientists have found that aerobic exercise such as running, biking, swimming, and skating causes the brain to release a steady supply of endorphins. This is because aerobic exercise is generally sustained for at least twenty minutes without rest in which time the brain is constantly releasing endorphins. As a result, people who participate in aerobic exercises have a high resistance to stress. A former substance abuser explains how running helps him: "When I'm stressed out, I go running. It's great. It gives me a major attitude change. The chemicals it sends racing through my body are pretty good too." [60]

Pursuing other activities

In addition to exercise, many former substance abusers find that participating in a hobby helps them to relieve stress and avoid a relapse. This is because occupying the mind helps people to relax while taking their minds off stressful events. Moreover, when people are busy their thoughts are less likely to turn to drugs or alcohol. Hobbies such as reading, gardening, painting, stamp collecting, music, and writing are just a few of the activities that former substance

abusers say help them to relax. One former substance abuser attests, "I have a flower garden. Working in it transports me to a peaceful world that's filled with wonderful scents and colors. When I'm working in my garden I forget about everything else. I don't think about work, or bills, or pills. It soothes me and fills me with happiness. It helps me deal with life's ups and downs in a way pills never did."[61]

Young offenders at a correctional facility in New York State jog together as part of their substance abuse treatment program.

Developing a support network

Another way formerly chemically dependent people cope with stress, emotional issues, and the challenges of staying drug and alcohol free is by developing a strong support network. In addition to attending twelve-step program meetings, many former substance abusers participate in electronic support groups, which they access via the Internet. These groups function like virtual support groups giving members a forum through chat rooms and discussion boards for sharing their experiences without requiring members to work through any particular steps. For people who live far from support group meeting places, and those who cannot get to traditional support group meetings due to poor health, lack of transportation or child care, busy schedules, or inclement weather, as well as those who are uncomfortable participating in face-to-face groups, electronic support groups provide members a chance to express their feelings while gaining information, encouragement, and a sense of belonging. In addition, members can access electronic support groups twenty-four hours a day. There are electronic support groups geared to accommodate every kind of person. These include specific support groups for recovering artists, lawyers, doctors, nurses, Christians, Jews, teenagers, people over sixty, and couples, to name a few.

Whether by participating in an electronic support group, exercising, meditating, seeing a psychiatrist, or avoiding old friends, it is clear that staying free of chemicals requires recovering substance abusers to make many changes in their lives. Though this is not easy, the outcome is worth it. A former substance abuser explains: "I thought treatment was rough, but the roughest part is staying clean. It's a lifelong commitment. There'll always be temptations out there. Remember the story of the snake in the Garden of Eden? Coke is my snake. It's waiting to bite me. I've had to totally change my life. I feel lucky that I had the chance. I'm alive and I'm clean. What more could a guy ask for?"[62]

6

Prevention

BECAUSE SO MANY lives are changed by chemical dependency, a great effort is being made to prevent new cases from occurring. In order to do this, authorities are taking a two-pronged approach. First, they are educating young people about the dangers of chemical dependency in an effort to keep them from trying chemicals. At the same time, federal, state, and local governments are passing strict laws to punish people involved in selling or abusing illegal drugs. The threat of going to prison, experts say, will prevent people from trying illegal drugs and, by arresting people selling illegal drugs, make it harder for people to obtain them.

Educating young people

There are a number of different programs sponsored by schools, the police, local communities, and various non-profit organizations that focus on preventing young people from using harmful chemicals. Some of these programs concentrate on making young people aware of the harmful effects of chemicals, while other programs concentrate on teaching young people acceptable ways to deal with peer pressure and other emotional issues. Two of these programs include D.A.R.E. and Life Skills Education. Lee Brown, director of the Office of National Drug Control Policy explains why he believes these programs are important: "I have always believed that the best way to combat drug use was to stop it before it starts. Only through early intervention can we instill in America's youth a set of values that will immunize

Schoolchildren in South Carolina kick off National Red Ribbon Week, an event promoting drug awareness. Such programs aim to prevent drug use through education.

them against the allure of drug trafficking and enable them to escape the misery of drug addiction."[63]

D.A.R.E.

D.A.R.E., or Drug Abuse Resistance Education, is one of the most popular substance abuse prevention programs in the world. Founded in 1983 in Los Angeles, the D.A.R.E. program currently reaches 26 million fifth graders throughout the United States and 10 million youngsters in fifty-three countries throughout the world. The D.A.R.E. program is a partnership between schools and local law enforcement agencies. Led by specially trained police officers, the D.A.R.E. program consists of a series of seventeen weekly classroom lessons that teach students skills needed to avoid involvement with drugs or alcohol.

The D.A.R.E. program teaches youngsters about the harmful effects of chemicals. At the same time, it arms youngsters with a variety of methods of refusing harmful chemicals and provides them with alternatives to drug use. This is accomplished through a series of carefully planned lessons that include role-playing activities in which students act out a variety of situations such as turning down a marijuana cigarette offered by a friend. These lessons help students understand the consequences that result from choosing not to use drugs. In addition, students are made aware of the peer pressure they face and learn ways to resist such pressure. Moreover, D.A.R.E. lessons build the students' self-esteem, while teaching them assertiveness skills that help them to refuse chemicals without embarrassment. In addition, it helps build decision-making skills and helps students to apply these skills in evaluating the results of risky behavior such as taking drugs. A teacher describes the effect of D.A.R.E. on her students:

> The students got a sound understanding of the many possible decisions they may have to face in their futures. The role-plays were great fun and allowed for practical hands-on understanding of situations. As the course moved on the children visibly grew in confidence and their conversations both inside and outside of D.A.R.E. sessions showed they really felt able to cope with any situation/decision they were faced with.[64]

Actor Erik Estrada and gymnast Nadia Comaneci pose with D.A.R.E. students. Students in the D.A.R.E. program are much less likely to smoke or use drugs.

A number of studies have shown that D.A.R.E. is indeed effective in helping young people resist abusing chemicals. An August 2002 study conducted by the Meharry School of Medicine in Nashville, Tennessee, for example, found that students who completed the D.A.R.E. program are five times less likely to start smoking than youngsters who did not participate in D.A.R.E. Similarly, a 2002 survey conducted by the National Institute on Drug Abuse found teen tobacco, drug, and alcohol use decreased for the first time since the poll was first conducted in 1975. Many experts attribute this decline to the D.A.R.E. program. According to former U.S. Drug Agency chief Barry McCaffrey, "The strength of D.A.R.E.'s organization is a major reason for our declining juvenile drug use rates. D.A.R.E. knows what needs to be done to reduce drug use among children and is doing it successfully."[65]

Life Skills Education

Another school-based substance abuse education program is the Life Skills Education and Training program, which is offered for three consecutive years to middle school students in grades six through eight. This program, which was developed by Gilbert J. Botvin, an expert on drug abuse prevention and a professor at Cornell University Graduate School of Medical Sciences in Ithaca, New York, grew out of a 1987 federal law requiring schools to teach drug prevention education.

Like D.A.R.E., Life Skills Training teaches students how to resist using illegal chemicals. However, the Life Skills Training program is led by a health or physical education teacher who utilizes a textbook, group discussions, lectures, and relaxation exercises to teach students how to improve communication skills, develop interpersonal skills, and cope with stress. Utilizing these important life skills helps teenagers better resist illegal chemicals.

The Life Skills Training program has been evaluated in over a dozen studies at Cornell University Graduate School of Medical Sciences. A 1999 study, for example, involved several thousand seventh and eighth graders in New York City, half of whom received two years of Life Skills Education and Training classes, and half who did not. The study found that

Former U.S. Drug Agency chief Barry McCaffrey laughs as Spiderman poses with two D.A.R.E. students. McCaffrey credits D.A.R.E. with reducing juvenile drug use.

the students who received Life Skills Education and Training were 50 percent less likely to engage in binge drinking than the students in the control group. Other similar studies found that Life Skills Education and Training classes reduced drug and tobacco use in young people by 87 percent, and the impact of the program is long-lasting. Because Life Skills Education and Training has proven to be so successful, the program was awarded the Exemplary Substance Abuse Prevention Program Award by the U.S. Center for Substance Abuse Prevention in May 2000.

Using the media

Unlike school-based programs such as D.A.R.E. and Life Skills Education, other programs sponsored by nonprofit groups, federal and state governments, and private businesses use the media as a tool for preventing people from abusing chemicals. Experts agree that the media has a powerful influence on how people view drugs and alcohol and their dangers.

According to a report on the Office of National Drug Control Policy's website, "Early research suggests that the mass media may have a role in decreasing drug use, and that the long-term exposure to anti-drug images, ideas and attitudes is needed to foster anti-drug behavior among youth."[66] Therefore, through billboards, websites, youth basketball backboards, and television, magazine, radio, and print ads, these programs warn the public of the dangers of substance abuse and, at the same time, promote the benefits of abstaining from drugs, tobacco, and alcohol.

National Youth Anti-Drug Media Campaign

One of the most far-reaching of these media programs is the National Youth Anti-Drug Media Campaign, which presents realistic depictions of the harmful effects of drugs and the advantages of a drug-free lifestyle. Started in 1998 and sponsored by the U.S. government, the National Youth Anti-Drug Media Campaign is a $2 billion media effort to keep young Americans from abusing drugs. Television, radio, billboards, and print media ads created for this campaign are estimated to reach 95 percent of Americans a minimum of eight times per week. Moreover, the campaign's advertising messages are presented in eleven different languages in an effort to reach and influence people of different ethnic backgrounds. In addition, the campaign hosts a popular website that has received over 15 million hits in the five years of its existence. The campaign has proven to be quite successful. According to Barry McCaffrey,

> Our National Youth Anti-Drug Media Campaign is working. The campaign's message is ubiquitous [found everywhere] in the lives of America's youth and their parents. From network television advertisements to school-based educational materials, from youth basketball backboards to internet web sites, and from local soccer competitions to national youth organizations, the campaign reaches Americans wherever they are—work, play, school, and home.[67]

Messages from celebrities

Another part of the National Youth Anti-Drug Media Campaign involves a number of celebrities speaking out against substance abuse. It is believed that their messages influence Americans of all ages, but especially American youths, to avoid using illicit chemicals. Olympic medal winners, professional athletes, sports teams, popular actors, musicians and singers, and television personalities have all made public service announcements alerting Americans to the dangers of chemical abuse. These celebrities include the U.S. Women's Olympic Soccer Team, the Cincinnati Bengals, the Los Angeles Lakers, Justin Timberlake, Jessica Simpson, and Matt Damon, just to name a few. In addition, acting as positive role models, many of these celebrities personally visit schools, churches, and youth organizations to promote substance abuse prevention.

An important part of these celebrities' message is their answers to the question, "What's Your Anti-Drug?" in which the celebrities explain what their dreams, hobbies, and passions are, and why substance abuse would stop them from reaching their goals. In fact, a 2003 celebrity calendar produced by the National Youth Anti-Drug Media Campaign in partnership with DKNY Jeans Company featured pictures of fourteen celebrities, such as Enrique Iglesias, along with their anti-drug messages. The celebrities' messages provide young people with alternatives to abusing chemicals, and encourage them to pursue their own anti-drug. Youngsters can submit their answers to "What's Your Anti-Drug?" at a number of special websites including Freevibe.com and DoSomething.org, and read messages from their favorite celebrities as well as from other young people. For example, television personality Yes of MTV's *Road Rules* left the following message: "I have a million anti-drugs! Break dancing, art, hip hop, skateboarding, my family, my peers, my girlfriend. There are too many to name. Respect yourself and your body. Drugs will never solve a problem. They only cause them."[68]

Using the law

Besides sponsoring the National Youth Anti-Drug Media Campaign, the government has passed tough laws to further discourage people from using illegal chemicals. These laws date back to 1969 when former president Richard Nixon announced that drugs were a major threat to all Americans' health and well-being. As a result, the government declared a war on drugs.

The war on drugs has two main thrusts. The first thrust is to cut down on the supply of illegal drugs coming into the United States from other nations, and the second thrust is to arrest and punish sellers and users of illegal drugs.

Cutting down on the illegal drug supply

Since many illegal drugs are grown in other countries, such as marijuana in Mexico, cocaine in Colombia and Ecuador, and heroin in Afghanistan, government officials think that making it difficult to smuggle illegal drugs into the United States will lessen the supply of drugs available in

U.S. Customs Service agents confiscate a shipment of marijuana worth $3.6 million. Customs Service agents work to prevent illegal drugs from entering the United States.

America. Consequently, the U.S. Customs Service and the U.S. Coast Guard routinely search seagoing vessels for illegal drugs. Similarly, the luggage of international passengers arriving in U.S. airports is inspected by Customs Service officers for illegal substances. When an illegal chemical is found, the person to whom the luggage belongs is arrested.

Also, Customs Service agents closely monitor the U.S. northern and southern borders. Five hundred specially trained dogs help customs agents apprehend drug smugglers at the borders. These dogs act as "canine officers" whose job is to sniff out drugs. In the year 2001 alone, canine officers discovered over 1 million pounds of marijuana and twenty-six thousand pounds of cocaine, and their alerts resulted in more than eight thousand arrests. Speaking on the success of these dogs, Jim Copulous, chief of the West Texas/New Mexico Customs Management Canine Program, remarks, "They've found drugs in tires, gas tanks, inside engine compartments and transmissions, every possible place you could think of in an automobile. There's no doubt in my mind that if the dogs hadn't alerted on some of these cases the vehicles would have been down the road."[69]

Even without the help of drug-sniffing dogs, the work of the customs officers is paying off. For example, during 2002 U.S. Customs Service officers seized 1.25 million pounds of illegal drugs on the U.S. southwest border. In fact, cocaine seizures alone amounted to more than twenty-eight thousand pounds. According to U.S. Customs Service commissioner Robert C. Bonner, "These cocaine seizures demonstrate that we have not wavered in our commitment to safeguard our nation's borders from drug smuggling. Drug smugglers pose threats to the stability and safety of our communities and the U.S. Customs will continue to meet these threats head-on."[70]

Strict laws

While U.S. Customs officers are confiscating illegal drugs and arresting smugglers on America's borders, local law enforcement agents are enforcing over fifty-five tough laws targeting the use and sale of illegal drugs in U.S. cities and towns. These laws require stiff sentencing for the possession or sale of any illegal drug, no matter the quantity. Consequently, even possession of a small quantity of marijuana can result in a five-year prison sentence. Similarly, illegal sales of alcohol to minors, for example, can result in the arrest of the salesperson and the business being shut down for up to six months.

Other laws make it illegal for people to smoke in public places such as hospitals, schools, and government offices, and a number of cities have passed laws making it illegal for people to smoke in restaurants. Moreover, zero-tolerance laws mandate that underage drinkers who are caught drinking and driving automatically have their driver's licenses suspended.

Many experts feel these tough laws have discouraged people from abusing illegal chemicals and indeed, use of most illegal chemicals is down. Moreover, tough underage drinking and driving laws have lowered the rate of alcohol-related car crashes involving underage drivers by 60 percent. According to *Dallas Morning News* columnist, Steve Chapman, "Alcohol-related traffic deaths have plummeted over the last two decades—thanks largely to tougher law enforcement. For a sixteen-year-old, the prospect of losing her license for six months sounds like a life sentence of hard labor in Alcatraz. Most teenagers prize their driving privileges even more than they like drinking."[71]

A legal controversy

Although these tough laws seem to be successful in lessening substance abuse, some people feel that the laws are too strict and should be changed. They cite the increase in the nation's prison population, which has more than doubled in the last ten years due to the number of prisoners serving drug-related sentences, and the resulting costs to society as one problem that these strict laws have caused.

Another issue involves the banning of smoking in privately owned businesses such as restaurants and bars, which some people feel infringes on the private property rights of the business owners as well as the patrons' right to use a le-

gal product in private establishments. Another law, recently proposed in Suffolk County, New York, has also angered a number of people. This law proposes banning smoking in cars carrying children under the age of thirteen. Opponents feel that the government is going too far when it restricts what people do in the privacy of their own vehicles. Even some members of the American Cancer Society oppose such restrictive legislation. "We do agree with the evidence that children should not be exposed to second-hand smoke," American Cancer Society spokesman Will Stone explains. "The difference is we don't feel it's proper to regulate environmental tobacco smoke in a private setting like the home and like the car." [72]

Police officers arrest a suspected drug dealer. People who sell or possess even small quantities of drugs can be sentenced to years in prison.

Drug testing

Despite personal privacy issues, the government is not the only group seeking to identify and prevent chemical abuse. Many schools and businesses require drug tests in which the urine of students, employees, and job applicants is examined for evidence of illegal chemicals. Traces of most illegal drugs remain in a user's bloodstream for up to a month, and like other waste products, pass slowly out of the body through the urine.

When a urine sample tests positive, the person may be required to seek treatment. In other cases, the person may be denied employment or fired from an existing job if his or her substance abuse endangers others. Institutions that require drug testing think that these tests discourage people from abusing chemicals because they do not want to suffer the consequences.

Many people feel that drug testing interferes with an individual's right to privacy and constitutes an unreasonable search. However, supporters of drug testing point to a 2002 National Institute on Drug Abuse study showing illegal drug usage to be down by almost 20 percent in the last six years as a reason to support the practice.

A lab technician tests urine samples for narcotics. Employees whose samples test positive may be required to undergo treatment or may even be fired.

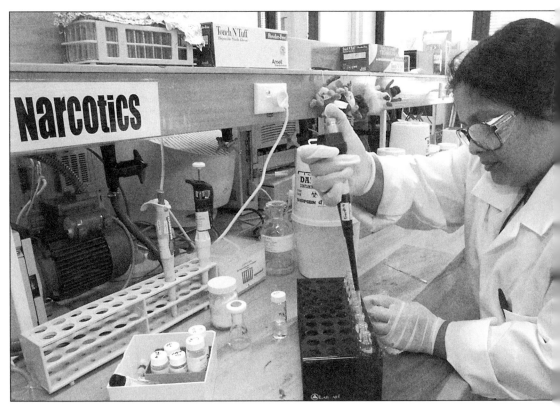

Clearly, prevention programs coupled with strict laws are preventing many people from abusing dangerous chemicals. As a result, experts hope that chemical dependency will no longer be a problem in the future. A former substance abuser explains:

> I'm not making any excuses, but if I'd gone through a program like D.A.R.E. or if my high school required random drug tests, I might not have started using. It was too easy back then. My kids have a different attitude about drugs than I did. The school and the TV tells them not to use and they believe it. It's great. Maybe by the time I have grandkids, getting high will be ancient history. [73]

Notes

Authors note: All last names have been omitted to protect the interviewees' privacy.

Introduction

1. Dion, interview with author, Dallas, Texas, November 15, 2002.

2. Ruth, interview with author, Dallas, Texas, January 23, 2003.

3. Dion, interview with author.

Chapter 1: What Is Chemical Dependency?

4. Vangie, interview with author, Dallas, Texas, November 10, 2002.

5. Dion, interview.

6. Dion, interview.

7. Elizabeth Connell Henderson, *Understanding Addiction.* Jackson: University Press of Mississippi, 2000, p. 63.

8. Henderson, *Understanding Addiction,* p. 53.

9. Travis, interview with author, Fort Worth, Texas, November 12, 2002.

10. Quoted in *Newswise.com,* "One of Five Children Will Try Inhalants." www.newswise.com.

11. Quoted in *EBSCOhost Electronic Journals Service,* "Hepatitis C More Prevalent and Easier to Contract than HIV," *Canadian Press,* October 2, 2001. http://ejournals.ebsco.com.

12. Dion, interview.

13. Anita, interview with author, Dallas, Texas, November 9, 2002.

14. Quoted in Janice Billingsley, "Teen Substance Abuse Could Increase Psychological Woes," *Yahoo News.* http://story.new.yahoo.com.

Chapter 2: Why Do People Become Dependent on Chemicals?

15. Travis, interview.

16. *BlueCross BlueShield of Texas,* "Why Kids Turn to Drugs." www.health.bcbstx.com.

17. *Elder Options of Texas,* "Alcohol Abuse and Older People." www.elderoptionsoftexas.com.

18. Quoted in Steven Stocker, "Stress Has Hormonal Link to Alcohol, Drug Abuse," *Washington Post,* September 3, 2001, p. A9.

19. Kelly, phone interview with author, Brooklyn, New York, November 18, 2002.

20. Quoted in Adam Marcus, "Attacks Spark Rise in Substance Abuse Treatment," *iMedReview.* http://imedreview.sub portal.

21. Connie, interview with author, Dallas, Texas, November 21, 2002.

22. Quoted in *Kids of North Jersey,* "Drug Abuse: A Personal Battle." www.kidsofnorthjersey.com.

23. Quoted in *Jewish Alcoholics, Chemically Dependent Persons and Significant Others,* "Pharmacy Drugs and Addiction in Jews." www.jacsweb.org.

24. Quoted in Adam Marcus, "Drug Use a Family Affair," *iMedReview.* http://imedreview.subportal.

Chapter 3: The Effects of Chemical Dependency

25. Dion, interview.

26. Shalaya, interview with author, Dallas, Texas, December 4, 2002.

27. Anita, interview.

28. Shalaya, interview.

29. Quoted in Al J. Mooney, Arlene Eisenberg, and Howard Eisenberg, *The Recovery Book.* New York: Workman, 1992, p. 534.

30. Quoted in *Angelfire.com,* "Thoughts on Grief After Suicide." www.angelfire.com.

31. Marvin, interview with author, Dallas, Texas, December 16, 2002.

32. Steven Belenko, "Behind Bars: Substance Abuse and America's Prison Population," *Casa Columbia.* www.casacolumbia.org.

33. Dion, interview.

34. Freeman Miller and Steven Bachrach, *Cerebral Palsy: A Complete Guide for Caregiving.* Baltimore: Johns Hopkins Press, 1995, p. 9.

35. *Babyparenting.about.com,* "Drug Addicted Babies." http://babyparenting.com.

36. Quoted in *Injuryboard.com,* "FDA Discusses Drug Abuse." www.injuryboard.com.

Chapter 4: Treatment

37. Henderson, *Understanding Addiction,* p. 91.

38. Terry M., "The Incredible Power of Denial," *Recovery & Sobriety Resources.* www.recoveryresources.org.

39. Quoted in *Intervention Center of Virginia,* "Intervention Frequently Asked Questions." www.intervention.com.

40. *Intervention Center of Virginia,* "Intervention Frequently Asked Questions."

41. *Spencer Recovery Centers,* "Saving Lives." www.spencerrecovery.com.

42. Quoted in John W. Maloney, *Intervention Center of Virginia.* www.interventionctr.com.

43. *Serenity Lane,* "Ten Myths About Alcohol and Drug Treatment." www.serenitylane.org.

44. Quoted in Marnie Ko, "No Excuses Here," *Report/Newsmagazine* (Alberta edition), vol. 28, no. 5, March 5, 2001, p. 62.

45. Mooney et al., *The Recovery Book,* p. 48.

46. Terry M., "What is Treatment?" *Recovery & Sobriety Resources.* www.recoveryresources.org.

47. Quoted in *Jewish Alcoholics, Chemically Dependent Persons and Significant Others,* "Blessed To be Clean!" www.jacs web.org.

48. Quoted in Mooney et al., *The Recovery Book,* p. 114.

49. Quoted in Mooney et al., *The Recovery Book,* p. 118.

50. Dion, interview.

Chapter 5: Staying Chemical Free

51. Dion, interview.

52. Dion, interview.

53. Quoted in Mooney et al., *The Recovery Book,* p. 169.

54. Mooney et al., *The Recovery Book,* p. 211.

55. Connie, interview.

56. Vangie, interview.

57. *Addiction Recovery Guide,* "Holistic Approaches." www.addictionrecoveryguide.org.

58. Quoted in Stacie Stukin, "Freedom from Addiction," *Yoga Journal.* www.yogajournal.com.

59. K. Sharma and V. Shukla, "Rehabilitation of Drug-Addicted Persons: The Experience of the Nav-Chetna Center in India," bulletin on narcotics, no. 1-004, *United Nations Office on Drugs and Crime,* 1988. www.undcp.org.

60. Dion, interview.

61. Vangie, interview.

62. Dion, interview.

Chapter 6: Prevention

63. Quoted in *Say No,* "D.A.R.E. Effectiveness Report." www.sayno.com.

64. Quoted in *DARE.UK,* "A Class Teacher's Evaluation of the D.A.R.E. Project." www.dare.uk.com.

65. Quoted in *DARE.UK,* "News and Views," www.dare.uk.com.

66. *Media Campaign,* "Testing the Anti-Drug Message in 12 American Cities." www.mediacampaign.org.

67. Quoted in *DARE.UK,* "News and Views."

68. *What You Need to Know About,* "What's Your Anti-Drug?" http://about.com.

69. Quoted in Brian Handwerk, "Detector Dogs Sniff Out Smugglers for U.S. Customs," *nationalgeographic.com.* www. nationalgeographic.com.

70. Quoted in *U.S. Customs Service,* "U.S. Customs Sees Dramatic Rise in Cocaine Seizures Along Southwest Border," press release, December 30, 2002. www.customs.ustreas.gov.

71. Steve Chapman, "Bush Girls Should be Thankful for Drinking Laws," *Dallas Morning News,* December 14, 2002, p. 31A.

72. Quoted in *ABCNews.com,* "Banning Smoking In Your Car?" October 11, 2002. http://abclocal.go.com.

73. Travis, interview.

Glossary

addiction: A state of chemical dependency. Addiction produces a noticeable effect on the body and causes withdrawal symptoms when the user stops using the chemical.

amphetamine: A stimulant that speeds up the central nervous system.

anabolic steroid: A drug that produces greater muscle mass and strength.

aromatherapy: A process in which people inhale warmed essential oils derived from plants believed to have tranquilizing and stress-relieving properties.

chemical dependency: A physical or psychological need for a chemical that is taken for nonmedical reasons.

cocaine: A stimulant that speeds up the nervous system and produces feelings of euphoria.

cortisol: A chemical produced by the brain that helps the body deal with stress.

D.A.R.E. or Drug Abuse Resistance Education: A drug abuse prevention program offered in schools throughout the world.

denial: A state in which chemically dependent people refuse to admit that they have a problem.

depressant: A drug that slows down the central nervous system.

detoxification: The cleansing of the body of the damaging effects of alcohol or drugs. The term is often shortened to "detox."

dopamine: A chemical manufactured in the brain, producing feelings of pleasure.

endorphins: Chemicals released by the brain, producing feelings of euphoria.

flashback: A side effect of hallucinogens in which hallucinations recur sometime in the future.

gateway drugs: Substances such as tobacco, alcohol, and marijuana, which are often the first chemicals that people abuse before moving on to more addictive substances.

hallucinogen: A drug that alters perception and causes hallucinations.

heroin: A highly addictive depressant.

hitting bottom: The point at which a chemically dependent person experiences a critical life-changing event caused by substance abuse.

hypothalamus: The part of the brain that controls mood, hormone production, and appetite.

inhalants: Substances that have a druglike effect when inhaled.

intervention: A process in which concerned people confront a chemically dependent person in order to convince that person to seek help.

joint: A marijuana cigarette.

junkie: A drug addict.

LSD: A hallucinogen.

meditation: A process in which people use concentration techniques to clear the mind in order to relax the body and relieve stress.

nicotine: An addictive chemical in cigarettes.

opiate: A highly addictive depressant such as heroin or opium.

outpatient treatment: A form of treatment in which chemically dependent people receive counseling and attend seminars yet may carry on their normal lives and live at home.

peer pressure: Pressure to do something that is placed on a person by his or her friends or coworkers.

post-traumatic stress: A form of stress that develops in people after witnessing or participating in a life-threatening event.

relapse: A condition in which recovered substance abusers once again repeatedly abuse chemicals.

residential treatment: A form of treatment in which substance abusers receive care and assistance while living in a treatment facility.

stimulant: A drug that speeds up the nervous system.

substance abuse: The abuse of dangerous chemicals.

tai chi: An ancient Chinese form of exercise that combines physical activity with meditation.

tolerance: Decreased response to the effect of a drug, causing the user to increase dosage in order to achieve the desired effect.

tranquilizer: A depressant that gives the user a feeling of calm.

trip: The experience a person has while taking a hallucinogen.

twelve-step program: A form of treatment in which substance abusers must work through twelve particular stages as they progress through their recovery.

withdrawal: The unpleasant symptoms people experience when they stop using chemicals they are dependent upon.

yoga: An ancient form of exercise that originated in India and involves controlled stretching and breathing.

Organizations
to Contact

Alateen
PO Box 862
Midtown Station
New York, NY 10018
(800) 344-2666

A worldwide organization that offers free support and information for teenagers who have family members who are alcoholics.

Alcoholics Anonymous
Box 459
Grand Central Station
New York, NY 10163
(212) 870-3400
www.alcoholics-anonymous.org

The central office of Alcoholics Anonymous helps people find local meetings. It also has pamphlets and official publications available.

Mothers Against Drunk Driving
511 East John Carpenter Freeway
Irving, TX 75062
(800) GET-MADD
www.madd.org

This anti-drunk-driving organization provides news and information about the problems caused by drunk drivers, provides support for victims, and campaigns to pass harsher laws against drunk driving.

National Clearinghouse for Alcohol and Drug Information

PO Box 2345

Rockville, MD 20847-2345

(800) 729-6686

www.health.org

A resource for all sorts of free information about alcoholism and drug abuse.

Office of National Drug Control Policy

PO Box 6000

Rockville, MD 20847

(800) 666-3322

www.whitehousedrugpolicy.gov

A large government organization and clearinghouse for current news on substance abuse. In addition, it provides a large number of publications, facts on different drugs, community support programs, and information on the anti-drug media campaign.

Partnership for a Drug-Free America

405 Lexington Ave., Suite 1601

New York, NY 10174

(212) 922-1560

www.drugfreeamerica.org

Provides news on drug abuse and prevention, memorials for drug abuse victims, real stories in multimedia, special information for teens, and an Internet newsletter.

For Further Reading

Books

Virginia Aronson, *How to Say No.* Philadelphia: Chelsea House, 2000. An easy to read book for young readers that discusses the consequences of abusing drugs.

Arthur Diamond, *Alcoholism.* San Diego: Lucent, 1992. A book for young adults that looks at what alcoholism is, its causes, effects, treatment, and prevention.

Elaine Landau, *Hooked.* Brookfield, CT: Millbrook, 1995. A book for young adults that talks about different addictions, including drug and alcoholism, as well as the effects of addiction and facts about recovery.

Wendy Mass, *Teen Drug Abuse.* San Diego: Lucent, 1998. This book for young adults deals with the problems of teen drug abuse. Issues such as drug abuse in schools, why teens abuse drugs, and drug testing are covered.

Gail Stewart, *Teen Addicts.* San Diego: Lucent, 2000. A book for young adults that presents real-life interviews with teen drug abusers.

Carolyn Kott Washburne, *Drug Abuse.* San Diego: Lucent, 1996. A book for young adults that discusses the war on drugs and deals with the causes, effects, and treatment of drug abuse.

Websites

CASA (www.casacolumbia.org). The National Center on Addiction and Substance Abuse at Columbia University is a combination think tank and action committee studying substance abuse and its effects on society. The site sponsors research and provides news items, connections to numerous links, and free publications and information.

DARE (www.dare-america.com). The official website of D.A.R.E. offers information about the D.A.R.E. program as well as helpful tips about staying drug free.

Do Something (www.dosomething.org). This organization helps people get involved in their community. Among the causes it sponsors is the prevention of drug and alcohol abuse. Geared to teens, the site provides real-life stories, contests, celebrity interviews, multiple links, and ways to take action in one's community.

Freevibe (www.freevibe.com). This is a national youth drug prevention website offering articles, links, information, and interviews with celebrities, all focusing on preventing substance abuse.

NARCONON (www.drugrehabamerica.net). A national network of drug treatment centers, which provides information on drug treatment and rehabilitation. The site provides research information, facts about thirty-one drugs, and a variety of helpful links.

National Institute on Drug Abuse (www.nida.nih.gov). This governmental organization provides a wealth of information on drugs, their effects on society, and prevention programs.

Sober Times (www.sobertimes.com). This nonprofit website gives information and true stories on recovery from substance abuse. It provides easy links to a number of twelve-step programs, as well as poems written by recovering substance abusers and an electronic magazine/newsletter.

Works Consulted

Books
Elizabeth Connell Henderson, *Understanding Addiction.*
Jackson: University Press of Mississippi, 2000. Discusses
what addiction is, legal and illegal drugs, why people
become addicted, and how to get help.

Freeman Miller and Steven Bachrach, *Cerebral Palsy: A
Complete Guide for Caregiving.* Baltimore: Johns Hopkins
Press, 1995. Although not about chemical dependency, the
book touches on problems in infants caused by substance
abuse.

Al J. Mooney, Arlene Eisenberg, and Howard Eisenberg, *The
Recovery Book.* New York: Workman, 1992. Provides questions and answers on recovering from addiction. There is also
a useful discussion about addiction and avoiding relapse.

Susan Newman, *It Won't Happen to Me.* New York: Perigee,
1987. Nine teenagers give their accounts of struggling with
chemical dependency.

Gary Somdahl, *Drugs and Kids.* Salem, OR: Dimi, 1996.
Examines the effects of chemical dependency on children and
teenagers. It also offers advice on how to prevent substance
abuse.

Periodicals
Steve Chapman, "Bush Girls Should be Thankful for
Drinking Laws," *Dallas Morning News,* December 14, 2002.

Marnie Ko, "No Excuses Here," *Report/Newsmagazine*
(Alberta edition), Vol. 28, No. 5, March 5, 2001.

Steven Stocker, "Stress Has Hormonal Link to Alcohol,
Drug Abuse," *Washington Post,* September 3, 2001.

Internet Sources

ABCNews.com, "Banning Smoking In Your Car?" October 11, 2002. http://abclocal.go.com.

Addiction Recovery Guide, "Holistic Approaches." www.addictionrecoveryguide.org.

Angelfire.com, "Thoughts on Grief After Suicide." www.angel fire.com.

Babyparenting.about.com, "Drug Addicted Babies." http://babyparenting.com.

Steven Belenko, "Behind Bars: Substance Abuse and America's Prison Population," *Casa Columbia.* www.casa columbia.org.

Janice Billingsley, "Teen Substance Abuse Could Increase Psychological Woes," *Yahoo News.* http://story.new. yahoo.com.

BlueCross BlueShield of Texas, "Why Kids Turn to Drugs." www.health.bcbstx.com.

DARE.UK, "A Class Teacher's Evaluation of the D.A.R.E. Project." www.dare.uk.com.

————, "News and Views." www.dare.uk.com.

EBSCOhost Electronic Journals Service, "Hepatitis C More Prevalent and Easier to Contract than HIV," *Canadian Press,* October 2, 2001. http://ejournals.ebsco.com.

Elder Options of Texas, "Alcohol Abuse and Older People." www.elderoptionsoftexas.com.

Brian Handwerk, "Detector Dogs Sniff Out Smugglers for U.S. Customs," *nationalgeographic.com.* www.national geographic.com.

Injuryboard.com, "FDA Discusses Drug Abuse." www.injury board.com.

Intervention Center, "Intervention Frequently Asked Questions." www.intervention.com.

Jewish Alcoholics, Chemically Dependent Persons and Significant Others, "Blessed To be Clean!" www.jacs web.org.

———, "Pharmacy Drugs and Addiction in Jews." www.jacs web.org.

Kids of North Jersey, "Drug Abuse: A Personal Battle." www.kidsofnorthjersey.com.

Terry M., "The Incredible Power of Denial," *Recovery & Sobriety Resources.* www.recoveryresources.org.

———, "What is Treatment?" *Recovery & Sobriety Resources.* www.recoveryresources.org.

John W. Maloney, *Intervention Center of Virginia.* www.interventionctr.com.

Adam Marcus, "Attacks Spark Rise in Substance Abuse Treatment," *iMedReview.* http://imedreview.subportal.

———, "Drug Use a Family Affair," *iMedReview.* http://imed review.subportal.

Media Campaign, "Testing the Anti-Drug Message in 12 American Cities." www.mediacampaign.org.

Newswise.com, "One of Five Children Will Try Inhalants." www.newswise.com.

Say No, "D.A.R.E. Effectiveness Report." www.sayno.com.

Serenity Lane, "Ten Myths About Alcohol and Drug Treatment." www.serenitylane.org.

K. Sharma and V. Shukla, "Rehabilitation of Drug-Addicted Persons: The Experience of the Nav-Chetna Center in India," Bulletin on Narcotics, No. 1-004. *United Nations Office on Drugs and Crime,* 1988. www.undcp.org.

Spencer Recovery Centers, "Saving Lives." www.spencer recovery.com.

Stacie Stukin, "Freedom from Addiction," *Yoga Journal.* www.yogajournal.com.

U.S. Customs Service, "U.S. Customs Sees Dramatic Rise in Cocaine Seizures Along Southwest Border," press release, December 30, 2002. www.customs.ustreas.gov.

What You Need to Know About, "What's Your Anti-Drug?" http://about.com.

Index

Picture Credits

Cover photo: © Andrew Brookes/CORBIS
Henny Allis/SPL/Photo Researchers, 68
Associated Press, AP, 43, 47, 55, 74, 77
Associated Press, Coeur d'Alene Press, 9
Associated Press, Kearney Hub, 50
Associated Press, Long Beach Press-Telegram, 52
Associated Press, Progress-Index, 83
© Annie Griffiths Belt/CORBIS, 44
© Bettmann/CORBIS, 19
Oscar Burriel/SPL/Photo Researchers, 26
Conor Caffrey/SPL/Photo Researchers, 56
© Robert Essel NYC/CORBIS, 28
© Image Bank by Getty Images, 39
Chris Jouan, 14, 24
© Liaison by Getty Images, 71
© Tom & Dee Ann McCarthy/CORBIS, 13, 37, 62
© News and Sport by Getty Images, 75, 80
© Jose Luis Pelaez, Inc./CORBIS, 67
PhotoDisc, 31
© Reuters NewMedia, Inc./CORBIS, 34, 84
© Chuck Savage/CORBIS, 27
© Tom Stewart/CORBIS, 64
Saturn Stills/SPL/Photo Researchers, 17
© Taxi by Getty Images, 41
© Jennie Woodcock; Reflections Photolibrary/CORBIS, 21

About the Author

Barbara Sheen has been a writer and educator for more than thirty years. She writes in both English and Spanish. Her fiction and nonfiction have been published in the United States and Europe. In her spare time she enjoys swimming, weight training, reading, and cooking.

362.29
SHEEN

DATE DUE

362.29   BC#004024044 $21.96
Sheen   Sheen, Barbara
                 Chemical dependency